TAKING APART
Bootstrap Theology

TAKING APART
Bootstrap Theology

Gospel of
GENEROSITY
and JUSTICE

TERRELL CARTER

JUDSON PRESS
PUBLISHERS SINCE 1824
VALLEY FORGE, PA

Judson Press has made every effort to trace the ownership of all quotes. In the event of a question arising from the use of a quote, we regret any error made and will be pleased to make the necessary correction in future printings and editions of this book.

Bible quotations in this volume are from the Contemporary English Version, copyright © 1995 by American Bible Society. Used by permission.

Interior design by Beth Oberholtzer Design.
Cover design by Wendy Ronga, Hampton Design Group.

Library of Congress Cataloging-in-Publication data

Names: Carter, Terrell (Pastor), author.
Title: Taking apart bootstrap theology : gospel of generosity and justice / Terrell Carter.
Description: Valley Forge, PA : Judson Press, 2021. | Includes bibliographical references and index.
Identifiers: LCCN 2020033371 (print) | LCCN 2020033372 (ebook) | ISBN 9780817018214 (paperback) | ISBN 9780817082222 (epub)
Subjects: LCSH: Church and minorities. | Church work with minorities. | Generosity--Religious aspects--Christianity. | Christianity and justice.
Classification: LCC BV639.M56 C37 2021 (print) | LCC BV639.M56 (ebook) | DDC 261.8--dc23
LC record available at https://lccn.loc.gov/2020033371
LC ebook record available at https://lccn.loc.gov/2020033372

Printed in the U.S.A.

First printing, 2021.

Contents

Preface

How people are perceived and treated by others is something that is extremely important to me. The reason for my concern is that I have spent most of my life experiencing the effects of other people's wrong perceptions about me and my twin brother and trying to push back against those wrong perceptions. We have innumerable examples of people in personal, professional, and religious settings making uninformed assumptions about us that have negatively affected us and made our lives and careers harder than they should be. Some of these negative perceptions stem from legitimate misunderstandings about us. Others stem from long-held racial and class biases to which people have knowingly or unknowingly clung.

For example, our mother and father were teenage parents, and neither graduated from high school. Although they were married, their union did not last, and our father was not an active participant in our lives until we were teenagers ourselves. Unfortunately, our mother, who had multiple run-ins with the legal system, was murdered when we were seven years old, and our grandparents, who themselves only made it to the eighth grade before they had our father when they were sixteen years old, accepted the responsibility for raising us.

Our grandparents told us that people assumed that because they did not complete their education and because he worked in a factory and she was employed in a domestic field, they did not believe in education or hard work, which was far from the truth. Through stories of their personal experiences of how white educators and police treated them like second-class citizens based on where they lived and worked, they emphasized the idea that we would need to be aware that people would make untrue assumptions about us and we would have to work twice as hard as others to be considered acceptable. We eventually learned that these types of conversations were not unique to our home. Most of our black friends were being told the same things by their parents.

Our grandparents raised us in north St. Louis's Ville neighborhood. The Ville was a predominantly African American neighborhood filled with homeowners that took great pride in their accomplishments, even though white politicians and police viewed the community as an eyesore. Our grandparents taught us that since we were young black men living in a black neighborhood, people would assume that we were not as intelligent as other children or as worthy of compassion. White educators who attempted to label me as learning impaired or my brother as combative proved my grandparents' warnings as correct. White police officers who labeled us as future criminals simply for being rambunctious children who played loudly with their friends also verified my grandparents' warnings.

Ultimately, what my grandparents helped me understand is that, in general, white people view black people differently than they do most other people. Our words and actions will typically be viewed through a lens of suspicion until we have done something to prove that we are not bad people. When a black person does something wrong, it verifies the suspicions that society has about us and feeds the narrative that African Americans are criminals and deserve to be treated differently than the rest of society. Because of this, police and other groups rightfully treat minorities in harsh ways.

This idea has been affirmed through the responses that followed the multiple negative interactions between minorities and law enforcement that have made the news over the past few years. These incidents have only added more fuel to the public debates about patriotism, nationalism, and the place and importance of race in North American culture. While the riots (some would call them uprisings) and unrest were occurring in Ferguson, Missouri, after Michael Brown was shot and killed by a white police officer, I heard a consistent refrain from black and white people within the St. Louis area.

That refrain was "I am not surprised." People were not surprised about the racially discriminatory findings showing how minorities were treated by various law enforcement departments in the region, or by how municipalities raised operating funds on the backs of citizens, or by how political and law enforcement officials from the region responded with false outrage and astonishment in the aftermath of the release of the Department of Justice's comprehensive report. The racial and economic issues that were brought to the surface in the aftermath of Ferguson exemplify the many systems that sustain the "business as usual" model that is found in St. Louis and other cities.

One of the things that did surprise me about the conversations that occurred during the Ferguson tribulation, although it should not have, was the participation of white Christians in the process of vilifying efforts to bring attention to the experiences and feelings of minority groups who believed they were once again being held to a different standard based on their skin color. Some of the questions raised by white Christians were these: Why are black people not more patriotic? Why are black people so unhappy? Why is it so hard for black people just to follow the rules? These are loaded questions. What do the people who ask these questions mean by "patriotic," "unhappy," and "follow the rules," especially when they are asked of people who have not always been considered fully equal to them or their ancestors?

These types of situations and conversations that will be raised throughout this book continue to remind the world of the racial and social dysfunction that is uniquely American. These are the reasons I find it important to write about racism and classism in America and the church's role in them. We, the church, tend to think and act as if racism, sexism, and classism no longer exist within the walls of our faith communities. This is partly because many of us do not experience racism or classism personally. We pat ourselves on the back when we have a few families of color within our communities. I think we would be better served by acknowledging that our faith and practice have often facilitated separation and political jockeying. Instead of denying the past, we can learn from it so that our faith can serve as a beacon for love and equality and living out the principles contained in God's Word.

I pray that by the time readers reach the end of this book, they will reevaluate the idea that a person's worth is based on thinking rooted in philosophy and theology developed during a time when all people were not considered equal even if they claimed Jesus as Savior.

Readers can find a Reflective Study Guide at the end of this book to enhance their reading and to challenge their thoughts, feelings, and actions about dismantling a "Bootstrap Theology." The Reflective Study Guide will also encourage the reader to explore their faith and reflection on God's presence and expectation for justice.

Ultimately, I pray that our beliefs about human value will be conformed to the spirit of God's words and intent, and not to a political or social philosophy. Thank you for joining me on this journey.

PART ONE

EXPLORING
Bootstrap Theology

CHAPTER 1

An Introduction to Bootstrap Theology

Aesop's Fables is a treasury of short stories attributed to the ancient Greek storyteller Aesop. The stories in the collection typically involve diverse types of animals that act like humans and face unique challenges that need to be overcome. Although each story contains both humorous and serious aspects, each ends with a lesson for its characters and readers that illustrates a universal moral truth that needs to be learned.

You may remember some of the moral lessons that come through the fables, such as in the story of "The Ant and the Grasshopper."[1] In a field one summer day, a grasshopper was hopping about, chirping and singing to its heart's content. As an ant passed by, struggling to carry an ear of corn to its nest, the grasshopper asked, "Why not come and chat with me instead of toiling and moiling in that way?" "I am helping to lay up food for the winter," said the ant, "and I recommend you do the same." "Why bother about winter?" said the grasshopper. "We have got plenty of food at present." But the ant went on its way and continued its work. When winter came, the grasshopper realized he had done no work and had no food and found himself dying of hunger. Eventually, he saw the ants distributing corn and grain from the supplies they had collected in the summer. Then the grasshopper knew that it is best to prepare for days of need when there is no need.

What are some of the themes found in this story about the ant and grasshopper? We see the idea of preparing ahead of time for what may come in the future; the idea of being responsible for yourself and how you spend your time; and the idea of learning to take care of yourself rather than looking for someone else to take care of you. These are the central ideas of bootstrap ideology.

You have probably heard the phrase, "Pull yourself up by your bootstraps." Bootstraps refer to the loops found on certain styles of boots that the wearer can use to pull them onto their feet. Although the exact origin of the phrase is unknown, one of its earliest uses was found in James Joyce's 1922 magnum opus *Ulysses*.[2] It referred to someone trying to do something completely absurd to improve their station in life.

In modern usage, it most often refers to an economic imperative that all people are expected to follow to be considered productive citizens. According to this imperative, all people have a responsibility to use personal determination to make sure their lives turn out well. People can expect to achieve certain financial successes as they consistently work hard and do not give up, regardless of external challenges. Success in life is achievable based solely on a person's willingness to put in the work necessary to achieve it. We most often hear this phrase within conservative political and religious conversations that espouse the need for all people to pull their own weight and not become a financial or social burden within certain communities.

What started out as an economic and social philosophy has morphed into a spiritual theology within Christian circles. When I use the phrase *bootstrap theology*, I am referring to the idea that based on a particular interpretation of the Christian Scriptures, the tenets of bootstrap theology have become part of how we understand our relationship with God and one another. As I will discuss in the coming pages, at its core, bootstrap adheres to the following:

- A person's value to God and their community is based on their willingness to work for what they receive so they do not become a financial and social burden on their community.

- God modeled this ideal by being the first being to work and produce tangible resources that benefited not only God but others.

- God requires that created beings follow the heavenly example that has been provided for them as it relates to a willingness to work.

- Although most people can work and produce resources that benefit them and others, some people choose not to.

- If a person is not willing to follow God's example of embracing work, that person does not deserve to experience the benefits that come from the work of others.

- A person's inability to positively contribute to their community is more likely due to their laziness or unwillingness to work than to the effects of any given economic, political, or social system.

Bootstrap theology recognizes salvation as a gift from God through the sacrifice of Jesus. Although there is the belief that salvation is solely a gift from God, those who receive that gift still have an obligation to actively participate in the salvation process by willingly embracing the gift that is offered to them and maintaining a lifestyle that proves the salvation gift is truly believed and received. This typically occurs through personal actions that help move a community forward spiritually and economically. If a person is not willing to do this, their salvation should be questioned. According to bootstrap theology, a person's willingness to work, or live a life that is filled with multiple types of work, is the primary symbol of their eternal salvation and placement into God's family.

This book seeks to explore how bootstrap theology has been used as a political and social tool by primarily white conservative

Christians and politicians to facilitate separation and fear among other white Christians within congregations and communities toward minorities and the poor in society based on a person's willingness to physically work hard or to live up to the standards those white Christians and politicians set for minorities and the poor to be seen as acceptable within society. Additionally, this book seeks to explore what it means to live in community, with all the diversity that can bring, in such a way that we regularly recognize that each of us is made in God's image.

NOTES

1. Aesop, *Aesop's Fables Together with the Life of Aesop* (n.p., Henneberry Company, 1897).

2. James Joyce, *Ulysses* (New York: Oxford University Press, 1998).

CHAPTER 2

The Foundations of Bootstrap Theology

Bootstrap theology finds its origin in the words of the apostle Paul in 2 Thessalonians 3:6-13. Within that passage, Paul sought to push back against members of that local body of Jesus followers who had, due to a faulty understanding of how they should live while awaiting Jesus' return to the earth, decided not to take care of themselves and instead depend on the kindness of others to get their daily needs met. In response to learning that this was occurring within the community, Paul responded with a clear command for those who were being lazy to get their acts together.

> My dear friends, in the name of the Lord Jesus, I beg you not to have anything to do with any of your people who loaf around and refuse to obey the instructions we gave you. You surely know that you should follow our example. We didn't waste our time loafing, and we didn't accept food from anyone without paying for it. We didn't want to be a burden to any of you, so night and day we worked as hard as we could. We had the right not to work, but we wanted to set an example for you. We also gave you the rule that if you don't work, you don't eat. Now we learn that some of you just loaf around and won't do any work, except the work of a busybody. So, for the sake of our Lord Jesus Christ, we ask and beg these people to settle down

and start working for a living. Dear friends, you must never become tired of doing right.

Biblical Foundation of Bootstrap Theology

The books of 1 and 2 Thessalonians were written by the apostle Paul to a small church in Thessalonica, the capital city of Macedonia, a Roman province. The city was situated between a prominent seaport on one side and one of the main roads that led to Rome on the other. This made Thessalonica a strategic city for commerce and a strategic place for Paul's missionary journeys.

In Acts 17 we read that Paul and his companions went to Thessalonica and taught several people about Christ being the Savior of the world. Through their efforts, many people were converted to faith in Christ. These multiple conversions did not sit well with the Jewish leaders there, and they began to give Paul and his friends a tough time. The Jewish leaders were jealous of the success that Paul and his friends were having, so they assembled a small group of people to falsely accuse Paul and his friends of saying that Jesus was a new king that would replace the current king. Eventually, Paul and his team had to sneak out of town in fear of their lives.

So this new body of believers had to move forward in the process of spiritual and communal growth without the people who introduced them to Christ, without interaction with their spiritual mentors. This process of moving forward was therefore somewhat difficult and messy. Over time false teachers sprang up among them and began to teach faulty doctrines that caused a major division in the congregation. In addition to that, this small body of believers continued to experience persecution from religious opponents who were jealous of their growth.

After leaving Thessalonica, Paul never forgot about this church, and he eventually sent people back to check on them and their spiritual progress. Reports came back to Paul that the church at Thessalonica was experiencing not only persecution from outside forces but confusion from within about what God was doing in their lives, the timing of Christ's return to move the church from the earth to heaven, and the eternal status of relatives who died before Christ's return. Moreover, they were frustrated and disappointed because it was taking Christ so long to return to get them.

Both 1 and 2 Thessalonians were written to encourage and instruct this group of believers as they waited for the day when Christ would return, which Paul referred to as the day of the Lord. "The Thessalonians had received some eschatological instruction while the missionaries were with them. They were taught to expect the Advent from heaven of the Son of God who had been raised from the dead; his Advent they would be saved from the end-time retribution to be experienced by the ungodly and would receive a share in kingdom and glory."[1]

With these two letters, Paul wanted to make sure the Thessalonian believers understood what the day of the Lord would look like, what would need to happen before the day of the Lord would commence, and what their responsibilities were leading up to that event. He hoped to clear up the debate in the Thessalonian church about how life should be lived in anticipation of Christ's return.

Some taught that Christ had already come, that the day of the Lord had already occurred, and they had missed it. And since they missed it, they could just give up and stop working and making a life for themselves. Others taught that since Christ's second coming was near, they did not need to work anymore because it would be useless to continue to try to build wealth and establish themselves in this world. Still others taught that it was unnecessary to work because Christ would supernaturally take care of his own people and provide them with everything they needed for life, regardless of the amount of work they put in. These were the conflicting opinions of how to live within a community that was awaiting the return of the Savior. "[The community] stood in need of further instruction about the coming Day of the Lord, and those members who, because of eschatological excitement or something similar, were idle and becoming a burden to their friends, required plain and stern admonition."[2]

In 2 Thessalonians 3:9-13, Paul wrote, "We had the right not to work, but we wanted to set an example for you. We also gave you the rule that if you don't work, you don't eat. Now we learn that some of you just loaf around and won't do any work, except the work of a busybody. So, for the sake of our Lord Jesus Christ, we ask and beg these people to settle down and start working for a living. Dear friends, you must never become tired of doing right."

Simply put, Paul told his readers that they should avoid being associated with people who live their lives in idleness, disorderliness, laziness, or loafing around. They should stay away from people who did not uphold the practices of working diligently like Paul and his companions. They should work for their own good and the good of their community. When a person worked, they could contribute to their family and community, which helped everyone. But when a person was unwilling to work or be productive, they were consciously taking from other people and placing an unnecessary burden on families and the community. This type of behavior was inconsistent with the example Paul and his friends set for them.

I can understand why readers may be inclined to understand Paul's words as implying that people within the community should regularly be doing something to take care of themselves and others. Taken at face value, Paul's words do seem to be saying that if members of the community were not busy being productive for themselves and their community, they would be disruptive and hinder those who were trying to be productive. Read this way, it would seem as if Paul was saying that there was no middle ground. A person would be busy doing one or the other—that is, they would be busy being productive or they would be busy making sure that other people were not productive.

Another way Paul's words could be understood is that being productive means carrying your own weight, getting in where you fit in, and finding a way to contribute to the overall good of a community. Being productive would benefit everyone involved. Any work that needs to be done is distributed evenly, and available resources are shared fairly and evenly. In this type of system, people help to take care of one another. But when a person is not willing to work, they are actively causing problems for everyone else.

Other people bear the brunt of the responsibilities and expectations to keep things running. Other people experience the physical and emotional stress of handling too many responsibilities. This interpretation—that a person has an obligation to follow God's example of working or producing resources that benefit not only themselves but other members of their community—is at the heart of bootstrap theology. Many of the commentators, sermons, and resources that address this passage from 2 Thessalonians convey that exact message. In doing so, they perpetuate and legitimize bootstrap theology.

Sociological Foundation of Bootstrap Theology

In addition to a biblical foundation, bootstrap theology also has a sociological foundation—the Protestant work ethic. The concept of the Protestant work ethic was codified by the German economist and sociologist Max Weber in his book *The Protestant Ethic and the Spirit of Capitalism*.[3] It is the belief that people who follow the God of the Bible should work and be engaged in gainful employment as part of their participation within a civilized society. This willingness to work is one of the primary means by which salvation is proven.

> If we now ask further, by what fruits the Calvinist thought himself able to identify true faith? The answer is: by a type of Christian conduct which served to increase the glory of God.

> It was through the consciousness that his conduct, at least in its fundamental character and constant ideal (*propositum obcedientiae*), rested on a power within himself working for the glory of God; that it is not only willed of God but rather done by God that he attained the highest good toward which this religion strove, the certainty of salvation. That it was attainable was proved by 2 Corinthians 13:5. Thus, however useless good works might be as a means of attaining salvation, for even the elect remain beings of the flesh, and everything they do falls infinitely short of divine

standards; nevertheless, they are indispensable as a sign of election. They are the technical means, not of purchasing salvation, but of getting rid of the fear of damnation. In this sense they are occasionally referred to as directly necessary for salvation or the *possessio salutis* is made conditional on them.

In practice this means that God helps those who help themselves. Thus, the Calvinist, as it is sometimes put, himself creates his own salvation, or, as would be more correct, the conviction of it.[4]

Weber understood that the practical application of Calvinism, which laid the foundation for a formalized understanding of works-based faith, had at its core the idea that a willingness to work was the primary way a person worshipped their Creator and expressed their faith in God. This expression of faith in God through consistent work was a key sign that a person had been truly converted and was securely included in God's family.

The idea that people should be engaged in meaningful work predates Weber's book, however. It existed from the beginnings of the Hebrew faith, which eventually influenced what would become the Christian faith. The Hebrew Scriptures begin with multiple stories of God working (creating). The primary point of the stories was that God worked to create things that were beautiful and beloved. God created the earth and other celestial bodies. God determined what it meant for there to be day and night.

Eventually, God created humans, the crowning achievement of God's creative work. God gave them a place to live, Eden, and in turn, a job to do. That job was to take dominion over all creation and represent God's interests for all that was created. This job included managing all other living things. In God's desire to have a clearly defined relationship with all that had been created, especially humankind, God initially gave only one prohibition. The only thing humans could not do was eat from a certain tree in the garden of Eden.

As the story goes, humans violated their only prohibition and ate of the forbidden fruit. In righteous anger, some may call it righteous love, God banished humans from Eden and pronounced a curse on them. Work would now change for them. It would no longer be a privileged part of their dominion over all God had created but instead would be a requirement for maintaining life. Work would no longer be only about intellectual stimulation (How much physical energy and labor was required to name animals, anyway?); it would now be a back-breaking experience. By the sweat of their brows and the strain of their muscles, Adam and his descendants would have to work to earn their daily bread and sustenance. They could look forward to physical labor until the day each of them passed away. Work would forever be viewed as a curse that could have been avoided.

As Christians have alternately viewed work as both a curse and a blessing, they have emphasized different views of the value of types of work. At various times, lesser value has been placed on physical labor, and intellectual labor has been more esteemed. Other times, intellectual endeavors have not been considered as valuable as physical labor. But one of the things that has remained consistent through these debates has been that a person's spiritual status is somehow tied to their employment or willingness to work. This idea carried over into the Protestant work ethic.

In *The Protestant Ethic and the "Spirit" of Capitalism*, Weber credited the theologies developed by Martin Luther and John Calvin, two Reformation theologians, as the driving forces behind the formation of what would eventually become the Protestant work ethic. "According to Weber, the Protestant Work Ethic was a construct of Luther, Calvin, and the Protestant Reformation. As Weber frames it, part of Luther and Calvin's theology was that hard work for its own sake was the core of moral life, a measure of worth and virtue, and a way to give glory to God. Labor was a means of salvation and wealth was a sign of God's favor."[5]

Martin Luther was an Augustinian monk who had become a leader within this new Protestant movement after becoming discontented with the actions and teachings of the Catholic Church at the time, specifically the Catholic Church's practice of selling indulgences—papers that promised salvation to anyone who would purchase one—to financially support the building of St. Peter's Basilica in Rome. Although Luther pushed back against these types of practices within the Catholic Church, he held too many assumptions that were common at the time. He believed that work was just one of the ways that people served God and the church.

According to Luther, work, which he referred to as "calling," provided stability to people and communities.[6] He also believed that divisions of labor naturally led to divisions of social classes. People were born to be employed in certain positions, and they should be thankful for whatever positions they occupied. Fighting against where God had placed a person in life was to fight against God directly since God designated every person's lot in life.

Where Luther veered from most theologians of his time was in his belief that all forms of employment, including manual labor, held equal spiritual value before God. He also taught that people should work to meet their basic needs and not work to build wealth or resources to hoard for themselves. According to Weber, Luther defined this overall "calling" as "an obligation which the individual is supposed to feel . . . towards the content of his professional activity . . . no matter whether it appears on the surface as a utilization of his personal powers, or only of his material possessions (as capital)."[7]

Although Luther was influential in challenging people to change their views of work, John Calvin has been thought of as having the greatest impact on the subject, primarily because his theology of work built on the foundation Luther laid while also expanding the subject and its implications. Where Calvin's theology of work primarily differed from Luther's was in Calvin's foundational belief in the concept of predestination.

In its simplest form, predestination means for something to be decided beforehand or for something to knowingly be set aside for a specific purpose or use. According to Calvin, God predetermined everything that would occur in this world. This predetermination makes God responsible for everything that happens. As this relates to humankind, on the one hand, God predestined, or predetermined, to forgive and save some people from suffering the eternal effects of Adam and Eve's original corrupting act of rebellion and disobedience recorded in Genesis and welcome them to heavenly eternal life. On the other hand, God allows those who are not predestined for salvation to suffer the consequences of their personal sin, as well as Adam's original sin, by being expelled to eternal damnation in hell.[8]

One of the many challenges that came along with this theology was the thought that God had predestined everyone to inhabit their individual stations in life, whether good or bad. The same God who made it possible for some mothers to adequately provide for their children was the same God who allowed other mothers to struggle to care for theirs. Calvin also believed that everyone has a station in life to fulfill. Some people are destined for much while others are destined for little. Every life is designed to fulfill specific duties. And everyone has a personal responsibility to play the part they are given.

One of the challenges with this type of thinking is a tendency to separate individuals from the overall family of God or their own communities and to see personal actions and attitudes as primarily affecting those who commit them or hold them without regard for how individual actions and attitudes affect others or interact with God's desire for justice for others. This idea will be explored further in the coming pages.

Calvin believed that persons should embrace those duties and fulfill them to the best of their abilities because their life circumstances are not due to any level of deserving or undeserving. They are simply part of God's plan for each individual. If a person can only obtain employment in low-level jobs, that is God's will for them. And if a person is able to ascend to a higher station in life, that is God's will. Since God is the One who determines every person's place, then it is God's will for some to be successful and others to struggle. Although God creates everyone, not everyone is created equal.

> While he [Calvin] is clearly aware that there are low-level workers in the community . . . he primarily treats the economic issues that face middle-class persons. He seems to write for the rising bourgeoisie, non-aristocrats who have suddenly found

themselves possessing a growing amount of worldly wealth and are in need of advice on how best to manage it. In his desire to set his theology apart from the Catholic mentality of his day, Calvin strives to help such people understand that they do not need to feel guilty for earning wealth through labor; but though they need not embrace a strict asceticism, they do need to keep their love for worldly goods in check. In order to motivate moderation in his listeners, he urges them to remember the people with fewer options than they, who might be victimized by the rapid economic changes in Geneva. He remembers the poor, certainly, but this is different than really involving the poor as interlocutors in his theology.[9]

Although Calvin believed that everyone has their own place in life, he did not believe that anyone is ever worthy or deserving of God's gracious act of forgiveness and salvation. No one is worthy of experiencing physical or economic prosperity. In Calvin's view, personal salvation and economic salvation are all gifts from God. And those gifts, both physical and spiritual, are not to be used solely for personal benefit. They are all to be used as part of the process to, first, glorify God and, second, serve one's neighbor.

According to Calvin, salvation and personal prosperity are not given simply for persons to feel good about themselves. They are gifts to be used to point people's attention to the One who has given them. This is one of the primary responsibilities of any believer—to make sure that life points to the creator of life. God's purposes for all people include them serving as God's representatives in this life, and if a person fails to do that, whether in regard to spiritual or material things, they are showing that they have not been set aside as a member of the coming kingdom.

Calvin saw every aspect of human life as a gracious gift from God; he declared that, having been redeemed through Christ, Christians were free from the need for righteousness under the law. Most economic decisions, therefore, were by and large matters of individual conscience as long as they did not offend God's laws, which included direct commands such as "you shall not steal," as well as the broader commands of Jesus such as "love your neighbor as yourself." Within such boundaries (and within the laws laid down by providentially-supplied local magistrates), the Christian has wide discretion over her particular behaviors. Nevertheless, her freedom is not unlimited but is bounded on all sides by the needs of human beings—both herself and others.[10]

One of the by-products of this thinking was the belief that a person had a religious duty to seek employment that paid well, because a well-paying job could allow the person to make substantial contributions to humanity and the coming kingdom through their finances. This theology helped to develop a mindset that saw work as a worthy way to contribute to God's plans for the world. And the more successful a person was in working, the more likely it was that they were able to contribute to people and the kingdom, and the more likely they were a member of God's elect. This also meant that any person who worked any job or made a financial contribution of any size—not just those with "good" jobs—could be in that "elect" group.

In some ways, Calvin's theology encouraged his adherents to see earthly success as a sign that God had chosen them for greater things. One of the few indications of assurance of inclusion in the kingdom was how well God was blessing a person physically and financially. If a person experienced a certain level of financial success, their success could be an indication that God was smiling on them and they were one of the "elect." If a person did not experience financial success and security, then it was likely a sign that God was not with them.

Calvin's thinking has continued to manifest itself and morph throughout history, and it has influenced many different attitudes and theories. One of these is the Protestant work ethic. A relevant example of this theory in action within the twenty-first century is the rise of Donald Trump as president of the United States. President Trump's public persona was built on the idea that he was a self-made man who pulled himself up by his bootstraps by following the mantra, "In the end, you're not measured by how much you undertake but by what you finally accomplish."[11]

Although my intent is not to demonize President Trump, his personal application of the Protestant work ethic serves as one of the clearest examples of how the theory has been used to separate people into categories based on who is worthy of justice, based solely on their ability to fulfill requirements that are believed to have been based on the Christian Scriptures. In the following chapters, we will take a closer look at other examples that show how the Protestant work ethic has been misapplied.

NOTES

1. Frederick Fyvie Bruce, *1 and 2 Thessalonians*, Word Biblical Commentary (Nashville: Thomas Nelson, 1982), xxxvii.

2. Bruce, xxxix.

3. Max Weber, *The Protestant Ethic and the "Spirit" of Capitalism and Other Writings*, ed., trans., and with an introduction by Peter Baehr and Gordon C. Wells, Penguin Twentieth-Century Classics (New York: Penguin, 2002).

4. Weber, 79.

5. Virgil O. Smith and Yvonne S. Smith, "Bias, History, and the Protestant Work Ethic," *Journal of Management History* 17, no. 3 (2011): 14.

6. Helmut Echternach, "Work, Vocation, Calling," in *The Encyclopedia of the Lutheran Church*, ed. Julius Bodensieck (Minneapolis: Augsburg, 1965).

7. Weber, *Protestant Ethic and the "Spirit" of Capitalism*, 54.

8. John H. Leith, *John Calvin's Doctrine of the Christian Life* (Eugene, OR: Wipf and Stock, 2010).

9. Kathryn Blanchard, *The Protestant Ethic or the Spirit of Capitalism: Christians, Freedom, and Free Markets* (Eugene, OR: Wipf and Stock, 2010), 46.

10. Blanchard, 10.

11. Donald Trump as quoted by Peter A. Laporta, *A Quote for Every Day* (Bloomington, IN: AuthorHouse, 2011), 166.

CHAPTER 3

The Problems with Bootstrap Theology

According to Calvin, one of the reasons for work is that it is an act of worship toward God. Furthermore, he said, the goods, services, or resources that come from work are to be used in service to others.

> Scripture . . . reminds us that whatever we obtain from the Lord is granted on the condition of our employing it for the common good of the Church, and that, therefore, the legitimate use of all our gifts is a kind and liberal communication of them with others. There cannot be a surer rule, nor a stronger exhortation to the observance of it, than when we are taught that all the endowments which we possess are divine deposits entrusted to us for the very purpose of being distributed for the good of our neighbour. But Scripture proceeds still farther when it likens these endowments to the different members of the body (1 Cor. 12:12). No member has its function for itself, or applies it for its own private use, but transfers it to its fellow-members; nor does it derive any other advantage from it than that which it receives in common with the whole body.[1]

Unfortunately, Calvin's good intentions have morphed into something unrecognizable. Our modern-day interpretation of the Protestant work ethic suffers from three challenges. First, modern applications focus almost exclusively on an individual's failure to secure financial security while disregarding systemic forces that contribute to poverty. Second, this focus promotes negative attitudes toward the poor, many of whom are minorities. Finally, modern applications fail to account for historical and/or contemporary circumstances that might prevent someone from being able to find work.

Disregard for Systemic Factors That Contribute to Poverty

While individual drive to achieve and accomplish may be admirable, that internal force is not always enough to get us to where we want to go in life or keep us there after we have met our personal employment goals. The families and communities we have access to, and the practices inherent within them, such as supporting others within that community or ensuring that resources and opportunities within that community are shared with other members, contribute as much to personal success as internal drive. Personal freedom to act is often supported by communal tendencies to facilitate personal and professional dreams and desires. The failure to recognize this reality is one of the primary problems with bootstrap theology. It is also one of the primary challenges inherent within white evangelical culture, which is both the dominant Christian culture in America and a hotbed of bootstrap theology.

Evangelicalism is based on the idea that salvation, participation in the family of God, is personal. One "decides" to participate in the process of salvation. This freedom to decide runs through all other life decisions. Success or failure in life is based on the personal choices one makes. Each person is solely responsible for how their life turns out.[2]

The following are four additional general characteristics of twenty-first-century, primarily white, evangelical culture:

- *Individualism.* Evangelicalism emphasizes a personal relationship with Christ through faith, prayer, and Bible reading.

One of the challenges inherent in this is that the outcomes a person experiences are the results of personal action.[3]

- *Anti-intellectualism.* According to multiple studies referenced by Emerson and Smith,[4] a widespread assumption within evangelical culture is that critical thinking (attempting to identify, understand, and engage with multiple sides of any given argument) hinders the gospel message of personal salvation. This results in a tendency to simplify any argument down to aspects of a person's personal salvation, which may lead to evangelicals oversimplifying complex issues rather than engaging in careful, critical reflection to more fully understand underlying issues, such as historic classism and racism.[5]

- *Anti-structuralism.* White evangelicals tend to emphasize personal accountability at the expense of understanding structural effects. This leads to thinking that whatever may be wrong in a person's life is solely due to personal responsibility. Evangelicals tend to underestimate the effects of legal, institutional, employment, and political patterns and how they set some up for success while hindering others. In evangelical thinking, centuries of societal structures should be easily overcome.[6]

- *Biblically based economic freedom.* Evangelicals typically believe that the Bible teaches personal responsibility as it relates to economic circumstances. They sincerely conclude that, based on what the Christian Scriptures teach, individual actions carry the greatest influence on personal economic status.[7]

One problem with this evangelical interpretation of Scripture is the tendency to spiritualize most life circumstances in such a way that even when Jesus clearly challenges his followers to understand the systems that cause poverty to better protect and provide for the poor, the reality of these systems are overlooked. This interpretation does not lead evangelicals to consider following

Jesus' example of reaching out to the poor to push back against the systems that keep them poor. Instead, evangelicals look for reasons not to help them. The very real physical and social barriers the poor may be facing become spiritual barriers that keep evangelicals and other proponents of bootstrap theology from helping them.

Another problem with this multitiered belief system is that it does not enable or encourage people to see the big pictures of structural racism and classism, historic intentional inequalities, and the effects each has on participants within our economic system. How can someone see the big pictures if they believe that everything a person has experienced in life is based on personal action or inaction? I'm not saying that this type of thinking makes evangelicals bad. What I'm saying is that it hinders them from understanding the experiences of people whose lives are vastly different from their own. "Though not necessarily intentional, the nature of white evangelical religion—with its inability to address fundamental and structural stratifications—has functioned to perpetuate racial barriers and systemic injustice."[8]

A final concern with evangelical thinking is that labor is never truly personal. In certain aspects, labor, an ability to work, is always communal and based on the opportunity someone else gives me to work. I can work if I am given the opportunity to be hired. I may have all the tools and desire to work, but if the person making the decision about who will get hired is unwilling to give me a chance, then I'm out of luck. If I desire to work but have not had the opportunity to gain certain skills, then too bad for me. If the person doing the hiring has preferences for employees to have similar experiences or backgrounds as theirs, then I will likely be denied the opportunity to be hired. I have experienced this firsthand.

Again, I recognize that for certain people obtaining work has never been a challenge. But for other people and groups, the aforementioned realities have hung over them for centuries. In the end, we can change our thinking about people who do not have the same life experiences as us. Their value in life is not based on what they produce or how often they make a positive social or economic contribution to our nation or our local communities. Their value comes from the fact that God created them in God's holy image and God's presence resides within them.

Promotion of Negative Attitudes toward the Poor and Minorities

Throughout his New Testament letter, James scolded a congregation because they gave preferential treatment to people who were well-to-do over those who were not. Specifically, in James 2:1-18, he chided his readers because they were treating the poor as second-class citizens and treating those of means as royalty. Of this text, Andrew Adams writes,

> James recognizes the temptation to favor people like us, or whom we wish we were, over against people whose affliction reminds us of how contingent our good fortune may be. This is just the half-hearted discipleship that submits to desire: the desire to be comfortable, the desire to be upwardly mobile, the desire to experience only life's ups, and to be insulated from life's downs.[9]

This illustrates another problem with bootstrap theology: looking down on the poor, many of whom are minorities.

We all struggle with being in relationships with those whom we consider poor. A better way to say it may be that we all struggle in our relationships with people whom we think are not as well off as we are. We struggle because we do not understand why their lives are as bad as they are. We want to blame them for their circumstances. We think that if a person would only work as hard as we have, or if they would have taken advantage of the opportunities they were given, or if they would simply get off their butts and try to work, then they would be okay.

This has continued to be a challenge for the church, especially as it has existed in the United States. We would think that it has not been true, but it is reflected in the thoughts shared by Christians through multiple surveys outlining their feelings about the poor. In one survey conducted by the *Washington Post* and the Kaiser Family Foundation,[10] Christians proved to be critical toward the poor because they thought being poor was due to a lack of morality. In an interview conducted as part of that survey process, Albert Mohler, president of Southern Seminary and a leading conservative Baptist leader, said, "There's a strong Christian impulse to understand poverty as deeply rooted in morality—often, as the Bible makes clear, in unwillingness to work, in bad financial decisions or in broken family structures."[11] The results of the survey reflect Mohler's thoughts.

> In the poll . . . 46 percent of all Christians said that a lack of effort is generally to blame for a person's poverty, compared with 29 percent of all non-Christians. The gulf widens further among specific Christian groups: 53 percent of white evangelical Protestants blamed lack of effort while 41 percent blamed circumstances, and 50 percent of Catholics blamed lack of effort while 45 percent blamed circumstances. In contrast, by more than 2 to 1, Americans who are atheist, agnostic or have no particular affiliation said difficult circumstances are more to blame when a person is poor than lack of effort (65 percent to 31 percent).[12]

A Christian's political leanings also influence how a person views the poor.

> Among Democrats, 26 percent blamed a lack of effort and 72 percent blamed circumstances. Among Republicans, 63 percent blamed lack of effort and 32 percent blamed circumstances. And race mattered, too: Just 32 percent of black Christians blamed lack of effort, compared to 64 percent who blamed circumstances.[13]

Somehow, politics seems to trump Jesus' words of seeing the poor as equally deserving of love and patience as anyone else.

This attitude can also be seen in the general makeup of any given congregation on any given Sunday. We feel more comfortable worshiping with people who come from the same socioeconomic background as we do. Craig R. Koester says, "Christians in North America may not think of social class as a problem, yet it is worth asking how comfortable the people in our congregations are when encountering people who visibly belong to a different social class. Networks of friendships often run along the lines created by income levels, education, and, professional status."[14]

We think that if God has blessed us to be gainfully employed, God can do the same for a poor person, if they really want it. We do not immediately account for other life factors that may have negatively affected a person's life or prospects. Instead, we think that if we and the people in our social group have been able to accomplish certain things, then anyone else can, and should, accomplish the same for themselves.

Even faithful Christians can fall into the trap of distinguishing themselves based on their life accomplishments and how those accomplishments afford them access to certain lifestyles and inclusion in certain groups. We learn to distinguish ourselves from others based on our social identity. Social identity is a process in which a person becomes aware that they belong to certain groups and that inclusion in those groups makes them better or more appealing than people who are not members of those groups.[15] Through social identity, we learn to distinguish ourselves from people whom our group deems unacceptable. We learn to keep our distance from the socially unacceptable and to hold them to a lifestyle standard that reflects our own values, experiences, and beliefs. Our realities become their realities, and if a person is not willing to conform to our conceptions of life and success, they become persona non grata.

Through the process of forming our social identities, we define the boundaries of in-groups and out-groups. Bruce Malina defines in-groups and out-groups this way:

An ingroup is a collection of individuals who perceive themselves to be members of the same social category, share some emotional involvement in this common definition of themselves, and achieve some degree of social consensus about the evaluation of their group and of their membership in it. A social outgroup is a collection of individuals who are perceived to be members of a different social category, to share some emotional involvement in some common definition of themselves, and to have in common a number of negatively evaluated traits typical of the group and of its membership.[16]

Those in our group hold positive traits that we are comfortable with. Those outside our group have traits that should be avoided at all costs. The members of the group we belong to are automatically worthy of respect, patience, generosity, and compassion, while members of the out-group are not worthy of even our time or general consideration. Much of our personal identity becomes wrapped up in how well our in-group is perceived and how poorly the out-group is described.

Also, whether we recognize it or not, many of us view our relationships with the poor through a racially and ethnically colored theory called the culture of poverty.[17] According to this social theory, poverty stems from multiple maladies believed to reside primarily in minority and immigrant cultures: poor work ethic, the inability of women in those groups to practice sexual chastity or to be married as part of the child-rearing process, an inclination to spend the money they do earn on recreational drugs and alcohol, and the propensity to regularly break the law. Our less-than-compassionate views of the poor and our interactions with them are heavily influenced by social ideologies like the culture of poverty theory.

Oftentimes we assume that a minority's level of poverty is likely due to inherent laziness while a white person's success is due to their workman-like dedication to becoming more financially secure. "At the center of the culture of poverty thesis is a binary; segments of the poor, racial minorities, and immigrants are positioned as having a deviant, morally suspect culture that undermines their potential upward mobility whereas white middle- and upper-class Americans are positioned as having a normal, morally upstanding culture that secures their class position."[18]

A culture of poverty perspective causes its proponents to hold a specific set of beliefs about the poor and minorities, most of whom we already anticipate will be worse off financially and socially because of inherent negative traits within their communities. We believe that political systems do not hold minorities back, but instead, by their personal and group feelings of dependence on government handouts and personal helplessness, minorities primarily live for the "now" and lack the skills and wherewithal to adequately plan for their futures. They lack a cohesive communal consciousness that would cause their entire people group to rise above their circumstances in life. For example, some people believe that minority groups are prone to having children out of wedlock because a preponderance of households are led by women who have loose morals, which causes them to regularly reproduce with men of equally questionable morality. In the minds of people who believe this, these factors make poor minorities less than honorable and less deserving of sympathy.

Failure to Consider Circumstances that Might Prevent Employment

I know multiple people, and you probably do too, who are currently unemployed. We all probably know people who go to church regularly and worship God with all their hearts, souls, and minds, yet they cannot find jobs that allow them to provide adequately for themselves or their families. This reality highlights a third problem with bootstrap theology: it fails to consider circumstances that might impact a person's ability to work.

We may have friends and family members who are not unemployed because they desire to live an unproductive life or because they do not feel like getting up every morning and going to work. They may be unemployed because of someone else's action or inaction that negatively affected their lives or because of circumstances that were well outside of their control. To understand this, all we must do is think back to the worldwide financial crisis of 2008 or the recent COVID-19 pandemic and its effects on countless people. The employment outlook for innumerable people was ruined. The financial crisis does not fully account for the many people who still cannot find or keep gainful employment because they have a criminal record that hinders them from providing for themselves and their loved ones.

If it were up to many of these unemployed people, they would not be spending their days in idleness. And for many, just because they are unemployed does not mean they are idle. They are not spending their time in other people's business as members of the Thessalonian church were. Instead, they are spending their time trying to find jobs, searching God's Word, and trying to understand why God would allow them to be in such dire straits, and trying to get back on their feet both physically and spiritually.

With that in the back of our minds, what could Paul be trying to say in 2 Thessalonians 3:6-13, which is so often used to support bootstrap theology? When I look at a passage like this, I try to see it from the vantage point of the recipients and let that clarify the writer's message. The vantage point of the Thessalonian believers was that they were waiting for their Savior to come back and get them. They were waiting for their Savior to show up and do something for them. They had placed their hope in Jesus returning and removing them from the persecution they were experiencing. Jesus' return would quell the fears they were experiencing from having lost loved ones that they were not sure would be in heaven with them. Jesus' return would mean they would no longer have to toil and strive for temporary things.

The downside to this hope was that the longer it took for Christ to come back, the more their faith waned and the more their fear grew—fear that they had it all wrong and that what they had trusted in was not valid. Fear that they had missed Christ's second coming because they had done something wrong and Christ had decided not to come get them. And the more their fear grew, the more likely it was that they would be tempted to turn their angst against one another. So they had to be aware of the temptation to take out on one another their frustration and fear of missing out on Christ's return.

Another vantage point of the Thessalonian church stemmed from their apparently being a tightly knit group who either wanted to take care of one another or felt obligated to do so. When necessary, certain people likely stepped up with extra effort when someone else would not or could not. Inequity in workloads was clearly driving a wedge between the members living in community. Some people who should have had one another's backs during challenging times were not carrying their share of the load, and that burdened other members.

Whatever Paul was saying to his intended audience must be understood within the context in which they were living—a context of hope and faith that was being stretched thin by multiple forces. Like the people in the Thessalonian church, we as individuals and congregations can, and do, struggle with remaining steadfast in our faith as life marches on. Circumstances that arise in our lives can cause us to question our relationship with God through Christ.

Where our lives should have hope and aspiration and celebration, sometimes there is only fear. Fear of what tomorrow will bring. Fear based on unanswered prayers and unfulfilled dreams and fear due to certain experiences that have shaken our lives. Fear that God is not with us like we have been told, or that God is not as close as we once thought. Whether that fear is founded or unfounded, it can stifle and cripple the strongest person. Fear can drive a wedge between the strongest relationships and minimize the most powerful faith.

But what is the antidote for the fear that plagues us in life? I wish there were a pill that could be taken to dispel all our fears and concerns, but there is no such magic solution. There is no quick fix, scheme, or formula for dealing with fear. The remedy for fear is to acknowledge it and turn it over to God and accept the peace offered through the Holy Spirit.

Bootstrap theology also fails to take into account that life in a community of human beings will always be flawed because someone will always be giving and doing more than someone else. Depending on where we each find ourselves in life, not every member of a community will be able to pull their full weight at the same time. At some point, one person may be stronger, more engaged, have more time and energy, or have more experience. The hope is that the level of commitment we each can display will regularly flow back and forth. That means that at any given point of any relationship, you may be giving and doing at a higher level, but at other times you may be giving and doing less than someone else. Hopefully, over time, someone else's efforts will increase and yours may decrease or vice versa.

Although it may sound trite, all I can do is repeat what God has promised us as God's children. God has said that, in general, we do not have anything to fear. God has said that we will be given what we need to endure the challenging times of life and to overcome them. Through God's mercy and grace, we will not be defeated by what life throws at us.

Conclusion

How people individually and communally respond to taking care of themselves or one another, and the potential fear that often accompanies such challenges is not new. How people could face such challenges without eventually seeing one another as enemies was at the heart of Jesus' ministry in the Gospels. In Matthew 6:25-34, Jesus clearly told his listeners not to worry about what life threw at them but instead to trust that God would care for them and provide for them, even if they or others could not work to earn what they needed.

Jesus spoke this passage early in his Galilean ministry as part of his famous Sermon on the Mount. The overarching theme of the sermon is trusting God while giving sacrificially of self to help others as an act of worship to God. The sermon is essentially a collection of Jesus' teachings on proper morality.[19]

The Sermon on the Mount begins in Matthew 5 with the Beatitudes—the "Blessed are those . . ." sayings. "Blessed are those who mourn. . . . Blessed are the meek. . . . Blessed are the peacemakers," and so on. Jesus used the Beatitudes to describe the character of the members of God's kingdom ("kingdom of heaven" in other Gospels). People cannot exhibit the qualities that are clear indicators of members of God's kingdom without help from God.

Another major teaching of Jesus in this timeline was the Lord's Prayer found in Matthew 6:5-15. One of the reasons Jesus gave this teaching on prayer was to push back against the practice of people making a display of their holiness to impress others. Taking Jesus' words at face value, it seems the habit of the day was to make a spectacle when praying or giving a gift. In so doing, a person brought attention to self to show everyone else how holy they were versus doing good simply for the sake of doing good.

As Jesus began to teach his followers how to effectively pray to God, he told them not to worry about what other people thought about them and instead to do their good deeds only for God's approval. In Matthew 6:1-6, he said,

> "When you do good deeds, don't try to show off. If you do, you won't get a reward from your Father in heaven. When you give to the poor, don't blow a loud horn. That's what show-offs do in the meeting places and on the street corners, because they are always looking for praise. I can assure you that they already have their reward. When you give to the poor, don't let anyone know about it. Then your gift will be given in secret. Your Father knows what is done in secret, and he will reward you. When you pray, don't be like those show-offs who love to stand up and pray in the meeting places and on the street corners. They do this just to look good. I can assure you that they already have their reward. When you pray, go into a room alone and close the door. Pray to your Father in private. He knows what is done in private, and he will reward you."

I think another reason Jesus taught this prayer was to affirm that God was the One who provided them with their daily sustenance, for he prayed in Matthew 6:11, "Give us this day our daily bread."

One of the things I understand about Jesus and his teachings is that he typically did not give a stand-alone saying. Rather, his words fell in line with a theme he wanted to emphasize. His words in Matthew 6:25-34 about not worrying fall into that category, for by telling his hearers not to worry about what to eat, drink, or wear, he was continuing the theme of trusting God that he emphasized throughout the Sermon on the Mount.

Those who considered themselves to be members of God's kingdom would need to learn to make God, God's power, and God's faithfulness their focus. And their lives were to be dictated by the reality of God's power and faithfulness instead of by their personal ability to make something happen. In Matthew 6:19-24, Jesus told his followers that their hope for life could not be found in the things they could accumulate through money or work. Those things were only temporary and would fade. Physical possessions could not be taken with them in death. And the possessions they accumulated on earth would eventually fight for attention against God, the One who provided those possessions in the first place.

Throughout his ministry, Jesus emphasized the idea that possessions and the opportunity to gain them were gifts given by God and not to be held tightly. Instead, possessions were to be shared among community members to make their lives better. The opportunity to work to gain something was not to be held over the heads of others. Instead, it was to be understood as opportunity given by God to make a difference for others. Work and the ability to gain the benefits of it were not the defining principle of being one of God's children.

One of the challenges everyone with possessions or the opportunity to work to gain them faces is to remember that the gifts and opportunities they have received from God are not to be held on to as if they will disappear. God has enough of both to replace what any of us gives away sacrificially. Bootstrap theology, however, espouses the idea that if a person does not work hard, they will not receive what they need in life, and the failure to work hard for what one has is sin before God. This idea stands in opposition to what Jesus taught. As Stanley Hauerwas said, "Abundance, not scarcity, is the mark of God's care for creation. But our desire to live without fear cannot help but create a world of fear constituted by the assumption that there is never enough. Such a world cannot help but be a world of injustice and violence because it is assumed that under conditions of scarcity our only chance for survival is to have more."[20]

Hauerwas's statement reflects the teachings of Jesus. Jesus wanted his followers to trust in him more than they did their possessions or their ability to gain them. He even went so far as to say that having possessions could make it hard for people to enter the kingdom in the first place because people tend to desire their possessions more than they do participation in the kingdom of heaven. Through the Sermon on the Mount, the Lord's Prayer, and his other teachings, Jesus was challenging his followers to trust more in him and God the Father than in personal work. He wanted his followers to understand that he was the embodiment and fulfillment of God's eternal promises to supply all their needs.

Jesus wanted his followers to develop a new mindset that since he was the embodiment of their daily bread that came from God, they did not have to hold on to things tightly or trust in things. Instead, they could recognize that through the abundance of God's gracious love, God would take care of them whether they had much or little. Worry about life and circumstances did not have to be their focus. The same holds true for us today.

NOTES

1. John Calvin, *Institutes of the Christian Religion*, 3.7.5.

2. Michael O. Emerson and Christian Smith, *Divided by Faith: Evangelical Religion and the Problem of Race in America* (New York: Oxford University Press, 2001).

3. Emerson and Smith.

4. Emerson and Smith.

5. Emerson and Smith.

6. Emerson and Smith.

7. Emerson and Smith.

8. Mark T. Mulder, *Shades of White Flight: Evangelical Congregations and Urban Departure* (New Brunswick, NJ: Rutgers University Press, 2015), 6.

9. Andrew Adam, "Commentary on James 2:1-10 [11-13] 14-17," *Working Preacher*, September 6, 2015, https://www.workingpreacher.org/preaching.aspx?commentary_id=2606.

10. Julie Zauzmer, "Christians Are More Than Twice as Likely to Blame a Person's Poverty on Lack of Effort," *Washington Post*, August 3, 2017, https://www.washingtonpost.com/news/acts-of-faith/wp/2017/08/03/christians-are-more-than-twice-as-likely-to-blame-a-persons-poverty-on-lack-of-effort/.

11. Zauzmer.

12. Zauzmer.

13. Zauzmer.

14. Craig Koester, "Commentary on James 2:1-10 [11-13] 14-17," *Working Preacher*, September 6, 2009, https://www.workingpreacher.org/preaching.aspx?commentary_id=384.

15. Vincent Yzerbyt, Charles M. Judd, and Olivier Corneille, eds., *The Psychology of Group Perception: Perceived Variability, Entitativity, and Essentialism* (Brandon, VT: Psychology Press, 2003).

16. Bruce J. Malina, "Who Are We? Who Are They? Who Am I? Who Are You? Explaining Identity, Social and Individual," *Annali di story dell'esegesi* 24 (2007): 103–9.

17. Jessi Streib, Saun Juhi Verma, Whitney Welsh, and Linda M. Burton, "Life, Death, and Resurrections: The Culture of Poverty Perspective," in *Oxford Handbook of the Social Science of Poverty*, ed. David Brady and Linda M. Burton (New York: Oxford University Press, 2016), 252.

18. Streib, Verma, Welsh, and Burton, 252.

19. Frank Leslie Cross, "Sermon on the Mount," in *The Oxford Dictionary of the Christian Church* (New York: Oxford University Press, 2005).

20. Stanley Hauerwas, *Matthew* (Grand Rapids: Brazos, 2007), 145.

PART TWO

DISMANTLING
Bootstrap Theology

CHAPTER 4

End Nationalistic Christianity

In Aesop's fable "The Fox and the Lion,"[1] **a lion has grown too** old and weak to hunt on the open plain. The lion pretends to be sick so the other animals will come to his cave and pay their respects to him as the king of the jungle. When the animals of the plain do come to his cave, the lion eats them one by one. Eventually, the fox comes to see the lion but greets him from outside the cave. When the lion asks the fox why he did not come in the cave to visit him, the fox replies, "Because I can only see the tracks going in but none coming out." The moral of the story is that it is always easier to get into a trap than out of one.

Something similar could be said of bootstrap theology: it is easier to get into the trap of this way of thinking than out of it. Maybe this is because bootstrap theology has become synonymous with Christianity in the United States and is largely accepted as being right. But as the previous chapter showed, bootstrap theology has serious problems. Nevertheless, even though it might be difficult to get out of the trap, it is not impossible. If we are to live in community and treat one another as Jesus desires, bootstrap theology must be taken apart. One place to start is by putting an end to nationalistic Christianity.

How Christians view the poor and interact with them is vitally important to God and to our Christian witness. How we actively live in relationship with the poor gives testimony to how seriously we take God's desires for how all humans should be viewed and Jesus' teachings about how the poor should be treated, not only within the future kingdom of God, but in practical daily life. We cannot claim to be children of God yet treat other people who also reflect God's image and likeness as second-class citizens based on their employment status, whether that status is due to their personal decisions or circumstances outside their control. As those who claim to adhere to God's principles of love, our obedience to those principles is clearly seen by how we treat the "least" among us.

I understand our behavior toward the poor to be influenced by our core beliefs about them and their worthiness to be included in God's family. Our actions toward the poor generally stem from our feelings that if we, as members of God's family, work hard, then they should too. We believe that it is not fair for them to experience the same benefits of membership in God's family that we hold so dear, or the benefits of living in the United States, if they are not willing to work as hard as we are. In many ways, we believe that salvation and citizenship are inherently tied to how well we publicly live our lives and produce tangible, meaningful actions and products considered valuable by others.

This train of thought is a fallacy. We are saved not by spiritual or physical works or by the things we produce in life, but by God's grace, God's unmerited favor. Because of this reality, the fact that our salvation is solely out of our control, we can rethink the connection between work, whether physical or spiritual, and our acceptability before God. And thus our thinking about the poor should also change. "[If] justification before God rests in absolutely no part on human action, then all human action is to some extent irrelevant to salvation. Good behavior is an addendum, a fruit, a by-product of prior assurance of one's salvation."[2]

As Christians in America, we seem to have forgotten the biblical principle undergirding Blanchard's words. This may be due to the tendency of American Christians to lean less on the Bible, which we typically claim as our primary guide, and more on political and social theologies.

American Christianity is old and pliable, and it tends to take the shape of the political or social party that holds the greatest influence at any given time in our country. Throughout our nation's history, Americanized Christianity has taken the shape that best benefits those who hold the greatest power to help them move their agendas forward. Americanized Christianity has been called upon to justify multiple atrocities that Jesus would have stood against, such as the wholesale slaughter of indigenous Native Americans, the enslavement and torture of Africans and their descendants, the forced relocation and incarceration of Japanese Americans, and the relegation of women to second-class status, to name only a few historical sins.

Christianity in America has regularly been used as a tool to force people to adapt to and align with the stories and desires of those in power. Whoever has the political and social power to shape the stories being told in our nation simultaneously inevitably shapes the meanings and ways of applying the stories the Bible tells. The stories they share from the Bible and Christian faith have consistently been that God wants what's best for our nation, even if the meaning of "best" is defined by only a small group or if only a small percentage of people will receive the "best" benefits. "The danger is that we can begin to read the Bible through the eyes of America rather than read America through the eyes of the Bible. We just want Jesus to be a good American."[3]

We shape our view of Jesus and the Bible, instead of allowing them to shape us, so that we are justified for the standards to which we hold others. This pliability of our application of the Bible is due to a lack of familiarity with what the Bible teaches, especially as it relates to human relationships in general, including God's desires for the poor.

Americans revere the Bible but are biblical illiterates. A Gallup survey found that less than half of Americans can name the first book of the Bible, only a third know that Jesus delivered the Sermon on the Mount, and 60 percent cannot name half of the Ten Commandments. Yet despite this current knowledge deficit, the Bible remains the central book of America's cultural and intellectual heritage. If one were pressed to argue for a single factor that has defined American Christianities, a strong case could be made for the influence of the Bible. To understand American Christianity, even American history, is to understand the history of the Bible in America.[4]

Due to this lack of biblical knowledge, American Christianity still often leads to groupthink about biblical principles. If you want to claim membership in the American Christian community, you must agree with the stories that the most powerful or influential in that community think should be told. Currently it seems that the biblical gospel, the good news of God personally working for the common good of all creation to make salvation (spiritual and physical restoration) available to all, is being replaced by a gospel of economic power and freedom, primarily for America. This new theology naturally leads to questions about who will be allowed to experience the benefits of salvation and community.

Our nation consistently clings to a nationalistic mindset that says a person's value is earned by achieving the American dream through personal work. This mindset also says that if a person is not willing to work, they should not receive any of the benefits that typically follow residency within our nation. This mindset also touts that although a person deserves to enjoy a full life if they are willing to work for it, they also must be the right type of person. If a person is willing to follow this creed, they can fit in. If they do not follow it, they should consider going somewhere else. This mindset was most recently expressed on a national level through the election of Donald Trump as president.

Although Donald Trump began building his public profile years ago by being willing to provide comments to the media on almost anything that was occurring at any given time,[5] his most inflammatory comments seemed to revolve around incidents that involved minorities. For example, Trump was not considered a legitimate political commentator until he began to publicly question whether President Barack Obama, our nation's first black president, was in fact born in America. He questioned Obama's citizenship as the first means to show his patriotism and concern for our nation.[6]

Another example of his divisive public statements about minorities is when he publicly called for the death penalty for the Central Park Five, a group of black teens who had been accused of assaulting a white female jogger in New York. When the incident occurred in the late 1980s, Trump went so far as to take out a full-page ad in a New York newspaper, expressing his anger and desire to see the boys receive the harshest penalty for the alleged crime. Years later, it was revealed that the case against the group of black men was built on less than a solid legal foundation, and they were subsequently exonerated of their charges and received multi-million-dollar settlements from the City and State of New York. Trump never recanted but instead doubled down on his original comments.[7]

Trump built his presidential campaign on trying to make some Americans fear those who look different, come from a different country, or have different life experiences from most Americans, even though those same traits are found in Trump's own family tree. This form of nationalism, the kind that supports only the interests of one's nation of origin to the exclusion and detriment of other nations or people who don't originate in your nation, was the platform that thrust Trump to the front of the Republican line. It also moved him to the front of the Christian evangelical line.

The nationalism that found traction through Trump is the kind that fears anyone who can be categorized as "other." This is evidenced via data that has been accumulated since Trump assumed office. Those who voted for Trump were more likely to hold negative views toward social minorities, especially African Americans.

Racism, and specifically anti-black prejudice, was shown to powerfully predict the Trump vote. Drawing on the 2016 post-election American National Election Studies, McElwee and McDaniel found that blaming African Americans for their soci-

etal disadvantages or feeling that blacks have too much influence in society were stronger predictors of voting for Trump
than economic anxiety or attitudes toward immigration.[8]

Before you think that I am anti-Republican, I acknowledge
that this unhealthy nationalism crosses political lines. It can be
found in circles that claim to be liberal or Democratic, as well.
Nationalism knows no boundaries, whether political or religious.

The primary underlying tool of this current form of nationalism is fear. Fear of the "other," fear of how our nation has changed
for the worse due to the inclusion of the "other," and fear of how
the inclusion of the "other" will continue to negatively affect the
future of our nation.

> Trump's Christian nationalist rhetoric also expressed a particu-
> lar eschatology of America's future, emphasizing how America
> was once a great nation, but had rapidly disintegrated under
> the influences of Barack Obama, terrorism, and illegal immi-
> gration. Trump's promise was to restore America to its past
> glory, a point he made most clearly with his ubiquitous slo-
> gan emblazoned upon red hats. The catchphrase has even been
> refashioned into a Christian hymn.[9]

I must acknowledge that not everyone frames the current incar-
nation of nationalism through the lens of fear. Instead, they frame
it through the idea of being "concerned." They say they are concerned that our nation and certain people within it are not living up
to their full potential. They are concerned because not everyone is
pulling their own weight. They are concerned because an increas-
ing portion of the burden for providing for the future financial
stability of our nation is being carried by fewer people each year.

In some ways, I can understand why some people may feel that
way. But is that the reality? Please do not misunderstand me. I'm
not saying that a person can simply be lazy and leech off others.
I do believe that we all hold a certain level of responsibility to
try to work and be productive. I understand that physical labor
is but one of the tools that God identified as being necessary for

the physical, social, and spiritual development of nations. I also believe that membership in God's family should bring with it physical and spiritual change.

The fruits of the Spirit that are outlined in the Bible should be readily evident in our lives. We should be willing to contribute to the spiritual and physical livelihood of our communities and local congregations. But grace and love—toward people whose life circumstances may not be exactly like ours—should be the first fruits we exhibit. Grace and love should cause us to view the poor in more compassionate ways—ways that Jesus modeled for us from the beginning of his earthly ministry.

Putting an end to nationalistic Christianity is one step toward taking apart bootstrap theology. My opposition to nationalistic thinking and bootstrap theology is not based on a personal belief that people do not have to work. My opposition is based on my understanding that this theology does not view all people as being equally valuable before God or that all people were created in the image of God, regardless of their life circumstances.

Any social or economic belief system that treats others as "less than" simply because of their life circumstances stands in stark opposition to the teachings of Jesus, the One whom Christians claim to follow. To truly follow our Savior, we should begin to care about everyone, including "the least of these" (Matthew 25:40). In the words of Stanley Hauerwas,

> Yet those who would follow Jesus are taught that we have time to care for one another through small acts of mercy because God's mercy is without limit. Abundance, not scarcity, is the mark of God's kingdom. But that abundance must be made manifest through the lives of a people who have discovered that they can trust God and one another. Such trust is not an irrational gesture against the chaos of life, but rather a witness to the very character of God's care of creation.[10]

Embracing Hauerwas's words is a first step to embracing the attitude Jesus had for those who are considered "other."

NOTES

1. Aesop, *Aesop's Fables Together with the Life of Aesop* (n.p.: Henneberry Company, 1897).

2. Kathryn Blanchard, *The Protestant Ethic or the Spirit of Capitalism: Christians, Freedom, and Free Markets* (Eugene, OR: Wipf and Stock, 2010), 24.

3. Shane Claiborne and Chris Haw, *Jesus for President* (Grand Rapids: Zondervan, 2008), 194.

4. Catherine A. Brekus and W. Clark Gilpin, eds., *American Christianities: A History of Dominance and Diversity* (Chapel Hill: University of North Carolina Press, 2011), 214–15.

5. Evidence of this tendency can be seen by a cursory reading of his Twitter messages found at Donald J. Trump (@realDonaldTrump).

6. A series of tweets stating his belief that Obama was not born in the United States can be found at https://twitter.com/i/events/77679561081 7007616?lang=en, accessed November 24, 2020.

7. Rebecca Morin, "They Admitted Their Guilt": 30 Years of Trump's Comments about the Central Park Five, *USA Today*, June 19, 2019, https://www.usatoday.com/story/news/politics/2019/06/19/what-trump-has-said-central-park-five/1501321001/.

8. Andrew L. Whitehead, Samuel L. Perry, and Joseph O. Baker, "Make America Christian Again: Christian Nationalism and Voting for Donald Trump in the 2016 Presidential Election," *Sociology of Religion* 79, no. 2 (Summer 2018): 149–50.

9. Whitehead, Perry, and Baker, 150.

10. Stanley Hauerwas, *Matthew* (Grand Rapids: Brazos, 2007), 146.

CHAPTER 5

Change the Perspective
on Race and Crime

One of the basic concerns most people have in life is their personal safety. In general, white citizens' stories about policing revolve around a long-held fear and distrust of minorities, especially those who invade their space. Some may disagree with this statement, but its truth is evidenced by a few things.

First, it was evidenced in the election of a president whose primary plank in his political platform was the promise to build physical and legal walls to keep out those who he, and others who think like him, didn't think deserved to be allowed into our country, as well as to deport similar people. Sixty-six percent of registered voters who supported President Trump in the 2016 general election described immigration as a "very big problem" for our nation, 79% of his supporters favored building a wall between the U.S. and Mexico, and 50% of those who voted for him believed that immigrants are more likely to commit serious crimes than Americans.[1] Playing to these types of voters, Trump played the fear card well and led to him being elected as the leader of the world's greatest nation.

Second, this long-held distrust is evidenced by the proliferation of incidents of white people calling the police on blacks because they didn't think the black person should be in their community or space. These types of interactions are the outgrowth of social and political beliefs mentioned earlier that whites must be protected from those who are "other."[2]

Too often the poor, especially those who are "other" (minorities and immigrants), are viewed primarily as suspects for potentially criminal behavior. As a pastor and former police officer, my experience has been that, in general, people find it difficult to show grace and patience to the poor, especially to minorities and immigrants, because we are inclined to perceive them as potential criminals. "Poverty is likely to be linked to crime both because the poor have greater incentives to commit crime and because poverty affects individuals' environments, their relationships, their developmental trajectories, and their opportunities as they move through different stages of the life course."[3] We often believe that poor minorities would rather take from others than work to earn their own possessions.

Pointing out the sins of others is easier than acknowledging our own sins or finding similarities between the actions of one group and our own actions or holding ourselves to the same standard to which we hold others. If minorities engage in certain behaviors, we say it is because they have not been raised well or they are naturally inclined to participate in certain detrimental behaviors. But if a white person engages in the same behaviors, we are more likely to try to find a legitimate or acceptable reason for their behaviors and seek to supply them with resources or treatment to help them.

We classify the actions that poor minorities and immigrants engage in as more abhorrent than those of others. If a poor black person or immigrant steals something to provide for their family, we criminalize that action in a way that we usually do not for others or for ourselves. Although stealing anything is wrong, if a minority or immigrant steals, we frequently call for swift and just punishment. But if an affluent white person falsifies their tax return for a substantial monetary return, we are more likely to look upon their action sympathetically because we frame it in a way that says it is acceptable to push back against a governmental system that overreaches on a regular basis.

Amid this groupthink, we can begin to understand that there is more to perceived criminal behavior than simply personal choice. "The field of criminology has a long history of locating the source of criminal activity within the individual. Without denying the importance of individual characteristics in affecting the propensity for criminal activity, and without denying the agency of individual offenders . . . the traditionally dominant focus on the offender has stifled progress in understanding variation in crime across places and over time."[4] If we are going to focus on potential criminality as a reason for viewing a person as being "less than," it is only fair to reframe the conversation so that it recognizes the equally unacceptable nature of all crime and potential criminality within everyone instead of primarily focusing on the crime of poorer minority and immigrant groups.

> The dominant focus of research in criminology and sociology places less emphasis on (or ignores completely) other types of less visible, underreported or understudied criminal activity or deviant behavior, including crime or abuse committed by police or elected officials' domestic violence, crimes committed in prison and many types of financial or "white-collar" crime. It is important to acknowledge that the disproportionate focus on what might be thought of as a "street crime" is likely to lead to biased conclusions about the overall strength of the relationship between poverty and crime.[5]

As in the example above of a poor minority or immigrant stealing to provide for their family, there may be legitimate reasons poor people commit certain crimes. Poverty, and an inability to overcome it, may have a direct effect on a person's options for sustaining themselves or their families in the real world. If a person is unable to secure necessary resources such as food, shelter, and health care on a regular basis, they may believe their options are limited to performing actions they would typically not consider under normal circumstances.

Instead of addressing the inequalities in the system, conservative and evangelical Christians politicize certain actions of poor minorities and immigrants to gain or maintain more political power over them.

> It is not surprising that the culture of poverty argument receives such long and widespread support given the functions it serves. Culture of poverty arguments justify exclusion, relieve agencies and citizens of an obligation to help the poor, and enhance the image of the middle class as morally upstanding citizens who deserve their class position. Policymakers can use the argument as a rationale to leave exclusionary policies intact; middle-class laypeople can use the argument to feel virtuous and innocent.[6]

This is most evident in the actions and policies politicians and leaders focus on.

> Contemporary calls for drug testing (of the poor who receive governmental benefits) and cutting food stamps echo elements of culture of poverty arguments—that the poor are prone to criminality, irresponsibility, and indolence—and that changing their situation through governmental assistance will not improve their outlook but make them worse. Policymakers' focus on welfare and inner cities also highlights who they think is engaged in a culture of poverty—the black.[7]

Again, I am not excusing criminal behavior. Instead, I am trying to get us to think about whether the actions that the poor engage in are worse than the everyday "smaller" indiscretions many of us participate in? Multiple studies show that if the tables were turned in our lives, we would likely find ourselves considering and participating in similar actions as those of the poor.

> A larger base of evidence suggests that unemployment (and underemployment or low wages) is causally related to criminal offending, with a stronger relationship between unemployment and property crime as compared with violent crime. This finding from the quantitative literature finds support in ethnographic studies arguing that the absence of stable employment and income are important factors leading to participation in

informal and illicit profit-seeking activity, ranging from drug distribution and burglary to participating in informal or underground economic markets.[8]

Sometimes it seems as though Christians are unwilling to show the same level of grace to others that they believe has been shown to them. We forget that all people hold common value, regardless of employment status, because God created them. "As creatures of God, all humans possess inherent value and dignity and are thus due a certain respect independent of any features or capacities that define who they are or even of what an individual may eventually become."[9] Unfortunately, many of us forget the inherent truth in the colloquial saying, "But for the grace of God go I."

We hold the poor to certain levels of moral responsibility to which we do not hold ourselves. We view them through the prism of our life circumstances and how we have handled what life has thrown our way, not realizing that their lives have likely been vastly different from ours. If our lives have been filled with fortune and opportunity, personal and professional connections, and supportive educational and economic systems, we believe theirs should be too. We forget that our lives have been shaped not simply by personal will but by the benefits that come with being born into certain families or communities to which some poor may not have had access.

A changed perspective on race and crime is a necessary step in taking apart bootstrap theology. This process begins when we start to recognize the value that all people have, regardless of life circumstances. This is a necessary step to seeing God's image reflected in all humans, regardless of their race or life circumstances.

NOTES

1. Carroll Doherty, "5 Facts about Trump Supporters' Views of Immigration," Pew Research Center. https://www.pewresearch.org/fact-tank/2016/08/25/5-facts-about-trump-supporters-views-of-immigration/. Accessed January 16, 2021.

2. Terrell Carter, *Police on a Pedestal: Responsible Policing in a Culture of Worship* (Santa Barbara, CA: Praeger, 2019).

3. Patrick Sharkey, Max Besbris, and Michael Friedson, "Poverty and Crime," in *Oxford Handbook of the Social Science of Poverty*, ed. David Brady and Linda M. Burton (New York: Oxford University Press, 2016), 627.

4. Sharkey, Besbris, and Friedson, 632.

5. Sharkey, Besbris, and Friedson, 624.

6. Jessi Streib, Saun Juhi Verma, Whitney Welsh, and Linda M. Burton, "Life, Death, and Resurrections: The Culture of Poverty Perspective," in *Oxford Handbook of the Social Science of Poverty*, ed. David Brady and Linda M. Burton (New York: Oxford University Press, 2016), 251–52.

7. Streib, Verma, Welsh, and Burton, 251.

8. Sharkey, Besbris, and Friedson, "Poverty and Crime." 626.

9. Kathryn Tanner, "Christian Belief and Respect for Others," in *The Politics of God: Christian Theologies and Social Justice* (Minneapolis: Augsburg Fortress, 1992), 166–67.

CHAPTER 6

Expand the Perception of Who Is Worthy of God's Love

A pastor friend of mine once said that people everywhere call somebody unclean. St. Louis Cardinals fans call Kansas City Royals fans unclean because of their rivalry. St. Louis calls Chicago unclean because of the Cubs and the Blackhawks. We all look for people whom we can cast to the outside so we can feel comfortable residing on the inside. My question for the reader is, who helps you feel like an insider? What person or group of people do you stand against to help you to find your identity? Unfortunately, American Christianity has a history of building its foundation on the process of describing and treating minorities and the poor as unclean. What will it take for us to end this practice?

As much as we may find sinners, the "other," unappealing in a spiritual and social sense, God overlooks their faults and finds them worthy of relationship. God's sense of who is worthy of love and compassion is vastly different from ours. Two passages, Psalm 32 and Luke 15, explore the idea of how we are to view people who we think are unworthy of God's love and our patience because of what we consider to be unacceptable actions: sin. One passage deals with how a person views himself as a sinner, while the other explores how others view certain people as sinners.

Psalm 32:1-11 reads like a confessional letter. The writer is clearly acknowledging that he has done something wrong; he has sinned. One of the theories about the creation of this psalm is that it was written by David after the prophet Nathan called him out for his sin of sleeping with Bathsheba, getting her pregnant, and then having her husband killed to cover up their infidelity. That sounds like sin if you ask me. And not just run-of-the-mill sin, either. That would be serious, grievous sin that affected many people in drastic ways.

Whatever the situation was, David acknowledged that he had done something wrong and recognized that he had brought displeasure to God. In the King James Version of the Bible, editors used a series of unique terms to describe David's actions and outline the seriousness of the situation. The KJV editors used the words *transgression*, *sin*, *iniquity*, and *guile*. *Transgression* means crossing a clear boundary to do something that is prohibited. *Sin* means missing a clearly defined mark by not doing what you know you should do. *Iniquity* refers to something that has intentionally been steered away from its intended path of travel. *Guile* means to do something through fraud or deceit. These are all words that carry the idea of actions that result in consequences.[1]

David's colorful language related to his sin did not end here. He said that as he tried to hide his sin and avoid the consequences, he felt worse about himself. He felt like his bones were weak and he was carrying a tremendous weight on his shoulders. His life was covered by a metaphorical cloud. David was acknowledging that whatever occurred, whatever happened, whatever went down, it was not by accident. He had intentionally done whatever it was that brought God displeasure and him shame. His actions had been unacceptable, and he was suffering multiple consequences for sinning and trying to hide it.[2]

But David's hopelessness did not seem to last long. After he finally confessed his sin, he gained a new lease on life because he knew that he was forgiven by God. God saw his sin, forgave it, and reminded David that he had not been left alone. Whatever it was that David had done was not enough for God to cast off

David. David was still God's child, despite his actions. Amanda Benckhuysen writes, "In other words, sin by itself does not necessarily determine one's status before God. . . . Instead, it is God's willingness to forgive and our willingness to receive that forgiveness that makes us right before God."[3]

In this psalm David acknowledged his sin and then sought God's forgiveness. He did not blame anyone else or push off responsibility for his actions on anyone else. And just as important, he did not try to compare himself or his actions to anyone else. He did not try to deflect responsibility from himself by saying, "Hey, look at what this other person did. What I did was not as bad as what they did." Do you know anyone who, instead of acknowledging when they did something wrong, pointed out the faults or sins of someone else? Instead of being responsible, they deflected by focusing on what someone else did?

We see some of that deflection occurring in Luke 15. The chapter opens with Jesus surrounded by the people in whose lives he was making the most impact—tax collectors and sinners, people who were on the outskirts of the organized religion of their day, people thought to be unclean and unacceptable. Certain religious leaders saw how Jesus was interacting with all these unacceptable people and scoffed at him. "He is a friend of sinners!" This was not a compliment; it was one of the sharpest barbs the Pharisees and religious teachers could have thrown at him.[4]

Jesus responded to these religious leaders by telling them three parables. The first was about a shepherd who left ninety-nine sheep that he had securely in control to go find one that had wandered away. When he found the sheep, he called his friends and neighbors to rejoice with him over recouping his loss. The second was about a woman who lost a single coin and turned her home upside down to find it. She, too, called her neighbors together to rejoice with her when she found the coin. And the third parable was about a father who had two sons, one of whom claimed his inheritance early and decided to go off and waste it. That father never gave up hope that his son would one day return home. When the son finally did return, the father invited his friends and neighbors to a great celebration feast. We know that parable as the story of the prodigal son.

What is the common theme of all three parables? When something important to someone has been lost, that person will go to great lengths to find the lost thing and will celebrate when it has been found. Ultimately, each of the parables represents God's love for every person and demonstrates how God celebrates greatly when someone returns to God's fold.

One of the overlooked ironies of these parables is that Jesus did not direct them toward the sinners and tax collectors that surrounded him. He directed the stories toward the Pharisees and religious teachers who attempted to stand in judgment over Jesus and his followers. This fact was lost on the Pharisees and teachers. They would never consider themselves lost. They thought they were the people who were closest to God. They thought they were doing everything God wanted. They assumed that if anyone was close to God, they were. So, as they were standing in judgment of Jesus and his followers, they were the ones missing the point he was making. Of this missed opportunity to learn, Justo L. Gonzalez says,

> From their perspective it was those others, the tax collectors and sinners, who were lost. So, the Pharisees and scribes would be unlikely to identify themselves with the lost sheep that the shepherd rescues or the lost son whose father awaits. They would see themselves as the 99 sheep, as the obedient son—and it would be shocking to see these sheep abandoned in the wilderness while the shepherd searches for the other one, to see the son missing the feast thrown for his brother. The parables would speak of the error of considering themselves faithful and obedient.[5]

Unlike David in Psalm 32, the Pharisees and teachers were unable or unwilling to celebrate God's willingness to search for, welcome back, and celebrate people who were thought to be lost. Sinners. They assumed sinners were off-limits to God's love and compassion. Jesus tried to tell them that this kind of thinking was wrong. Scott Hoezee writes,

Indeed, when you serve a stingy and joyless God, you assume that this is a God who has to work extra hard just to love YOU. It's a cinch then to assume that this same God hates people "out there" in the world who don't even look remotely religious. And since not getting caught up in their ways—or contaminated by their spiritual germs—is your primary goal, you avoid, you shun, you judge from afar. What you most certainly do NOT do, however, is sit at table with those greasy characters (as Jesus did).[6]

Please do not mistake my words. I believe that sin is sin is sin is sin. It grieves God's heart and is the opposite of what God wants. But sin, regardless of the form we think it takes, is not the final arbitrator of God's relationship with people. God's love for David, for tax collectors and sinners, and even for us is greater than we can imagine. God's love is so great that God sent the Son to take away the sins of the world. David, tax collectors, and sinners, and even we, are forgiven of our sins.

We are made right before God not through our works or our employment but through the work of God's Son. God's love for a person is not based on their employment status or their willingness to labor for a set number of hours every day. Our participation in God's kingdom is based on God's undying love for God's creation and God's desire to return to a proper relationship with all that God has created.

This is part of the challenge we face when we view God's love through the prism of work and bootstrap theology. When we view it through that lens, we forget that nothing we do is valuable enough or worth enough to earn God's love, and we forget that God's greatest sign of approval toward us is not physical blessings or temporary possessions. The greatest sign is the redemptive sacrifice that was made for us by our Savior. Since we all possess God-approved value, viewing one another through the lens of bootstrap theology diminishes God's intentions for our relationships.

When we follow bootstrap theology, we are attempting to determine who is in or out and who deserves or does not deserve our respect, mercy, or love. We use bootstrap theology to categorize who we think is worthy of God's respect or mercy or love. Ultimately, we use bootstrap theology to describe who we think is a part of God's family and who is not. When we do that, we fail to remember that God calls us to reach out to those who we think are unclean or unworthy of our time and compassion. We forget that God's Spirit seeks to send us to people who need to understand that God loves them and wants to be in relationship with them just as they are and right where they are located. Bootstrap theology causes us to forget that God's love overcomes uncleanness and otherness.

NOTES

1. Nancy L. deClaisse-Walford, Rolf A. Jacobson, and Beth LaNeel Tanner, *The Book of Psalms* (Grand Rapids: Eerdmans, 2014).

2. deClaisse-Walford, Jacobson, and Tanner.

3. Amanda Benckhuysen, "Commentary on Psalm 32," Working Preacher, March 31, 2019, https://www.workingpreacher.org/preaching. aspx?commentary_id=4000.

4. Darrell Bock, *Luke* (Grand Rapids: Baker Academic, 1996).

5. Justo Gonzalez, "What If We Are the Pharisees?" *The Christian Century*, February 26, 2019, https://www.christiancentury.org/article/ living-word/march-31-lent-4c-luke-151-3-11b-32.

6. Scott Hoezee, "Commentary on Luke 15:1-2, 11-32," Center for Excellence in Preaching, February 29, 2016, https://cep.calvinseminary. edu/sermon-starters/lent-4c/.

PART THREE

REPLACING
Bootstrap Theology
with a Gospel
of Generosity
and Justice

CHAPTER 7

A Biblically Faithful View of Wealth and Poverty

The musical *Big River: The Adventures of Huckleberry Finn* is one of my favorite Broadway musicals. It is based on the 1884 book *The Adventures of Huckleberry Finn* by Mark Twain. The book and musical tell the story of Huckleberry Finn, Tom Sawyer, and a runaway slave named Jim and their adventures along the Mississippi River during the late nineteenth century. The storyline of *Huckleberry Finn* explores multiple unfulfilled dreams.

As the book and musical open, Huck has been adopted by two older women, and they are set on civilizing him and saving his soul. Instead of being civilized and saved, Huck dreams of adventure and love. Jim, the slave, struggles with civilization and salvation of a different kind. He dreams of being treated in a civilized manner by people who do not see him as fully human. He dreams of equality and opportunity.

The crowning song of the musical, in my opinion, is titled "Worlds Apart." Although the two main characters were worlds apart due to their races and economic standings, both characters held on to a common hope—to be free. Free of others' expectations of them. Free of the physical confines they both faced. As they struggled with the idea of freedom, they also had to face other pressing questions. Some of those questions came from within themselves while other questions came from without. Questions like, is life fair? Did God create all people to be equal? If God did, then why are some people not treated that way?

Huck, the boy of adventure, also had to deal with the question of whether he was willing to be made into a civilized young man by the women in his life who cared for him, as well as by the townspeople. Jim had to deal with the question of whether he would allow himself to continue being treated as "other." Would he allow himself to be sold to yet another master who would not treat him well? Neither waited for someone else to give him the answers to his questions. Both escaped their circumstances and floated down the Mississippi River toward freedom—physical and psychological freedom.

Throughout the musical and book, the theme of slave and free, the haves and have-nots, rich and poor, are explored. These themes are most clearly understood through the juxtaposition of Huck, the free white teen, and Jim, the enslaved black man. As part of considering these themes, the musical does a commendable job of asking questions that challenge viewers to begin to view each man as equal. Questions like, are we obligated to view someone in the same way the rest of society views them? In multiple places, the Bible asks us the same types of questions, especially as it relates to those we consider "other." I believe the Bible does this because it is an important question to God.

The relationship between the rich and poor, those who have more than enough and those who do not, is important to God—so much so that this relationship is addressed in multiple places in the Bible. In the Hebrew Scriptures, God told the children of Israel that when they finally entered the Promised Land, the land that symbolized God's faithfulness to fulfill generations-old promises to take care of them through a land where, by God's grace, all of their physical needs would be met, they were to remember that they had once been slaves who did not have enough (see Deuteronomy 15:15).

On multiple occasions, God commanded the Israelites to remember this because they, too, would encounter people who, after God's people had taken over the Promised Land, would not have enough to cover some of their basic daily needs (see Exodus 22:21 and 23:9). In honor of God's faithfulness in providing for the children of Israel, they were not to hoard all the fruit the land produced for themselves. Instead, they were to forgo reaping every piece of fruit and grain and leave some of the excesses the land produced to be reaped by the poor and hungry from their own tribes, as well as from other nations, to use for their own needs.

Jesus frequently talked about the relationships between the rich and poor. He regularly challenged those who had enough to share with those who did not have much (see Matthew 19:16-30). Several times Jesus lauded the strength and faithfulness of the poor, declaring that those who did not have much in the here and now would be given more than they could imagine in the coming kingdom (see Luke 6:20-21). And those who currently had more than enough would experience a reversal of fortunes when the new kingdom became visible. He also shared a parable in which the rich were challenged to loosen their grip on possessions and instead embrace people more intently (see Luke 12:13-21).

Following Jesus' example, the church should care about the poor in tangible ways. Martin Luther King Jr. expressed this truth eloquently when he wrote,

> The Christian ought always to be challenged by any protest against unfair treatment of the poor, for Christianity is itself such a protest, nowhere expressed more eloquently than in Jesus' words: "The Spirit of the Lord is upon me, because he hath anointed me to preach the gospel to the poor; he hath sent me to heal the broken hearted, to preach deliverance to captives, and recovering of sight to the blind, to set at liberty them that are bruised, to preach the acceptable year of the Lord."[1]

In so many ways, our contemporary views of wealth and poverty and of the social status of those who reside on the multiple points of the wealth spectrum stand in stark contrast to Dr. King's words and the clear teachings of the Bible. The Old Testament prophets encouraged us not to put our trust in monetary wealth or physical possessions but instead to see our possessions as tools that God can use to care for others (see Amos, especially chapters 3 and 6, and Micah 2). Jesus stressed in multiple parables the futility of putting trust in possessions and money rather than in the One who made it possible to obtain possessions and money (see Luke 12:13-21). The New Testament writers also warned about placing too much value on possessions and money and not enough value on people and relationships (see Acts 2, Hebrews 10:34, and 1 John 3:17).

James, the brother of Jesus and leader within the fledgling church, remembered Jesus' words about how to treat the poor and reflected them in the teachings he penned to the early church. His words, especially those found in James 5:1-6, clearly show that viewing the poor in a negative way is inconsistent with the types of relationships God hopes for God's people to experience. James plainly declared that those who treat the rich and poor differently would be held accountable by God for their actions.

The Bible never says that it is wrong to be rich, to have wealth, or to be successful in business. Possessing wealth does not automatically equal separation from God or God's community. What the Bible does say in various ways is that placing an unhealthy emphasis on earning, maintaining, and protecting money and possessions typically leads to an unhealthy perspective and trust in those material things and a corresponding lack of concern for other people. When someone makes money or possessions their focus, there is the distinct possibility that God and God's desires will take a back seat in that person's life.

Although the Bible does not identify having wealth as an outright sin, the Bible does take a specific view of relationships between those who have financial means and those who do not. These relationships are often described in terms of rich and poor, and they underlie much of the Hebrew Bible. George Peck writes, "Though the Old Testament by no means glorifies poverty as a good thing in itself, many strands of Israel's literary tradition plainly depict God as unequivocally on the side of the poor."[2]

Why did God intentionally, and most times very vocally, side with the poor in the Old Testament? Because the poor understood that their help, protection, sustenance, provisions, and hope came from outside themselves. They came from God. The rich, on the other hand, typically gave themselves credit for any success they experienced and believed that their wealth and wisdom would get them out of any troublesome life circumstances.

According to the Old Testament, not only were the poor held in high esteem by God, but those who helped, supported, and protected the poor were either on God's side or experienced God's favor. Alternatively, if you were not a friend of the poor, you were not a friend of God. Peck continues, "As the poor are 'friends of God,' so also are those who are concerned for them; but the enemies of the poor are ipso facto enemies of the Lord and in God's ordering of things will be treated as such."[3]

In his letter to the church, James recognized the temptation that all people face to view the poor as expendable and the rich as worthy of honor. We typically base this type of thinking on what we see a person wearing or driving or on the types of spaces they occupy. If they wear designer clothes or drive an expensive car, we automatically believe that person is successful and that their success came from their hard work and dedication. We then believe their success earns them special privileges like preferential seating within religious spaces, which was the case for the group James's letter was addressed to.

When these well-to-do people showed up to participate in corporate worship, they were treated like royalty, while those of humble means were directed to make space for the rich. Deferring to someone based on their economic status violated the spirit and intent of living in the world but not being of it. Peck writes,

For James the Christian community is made up chiefly of poor people. This is as it should be, given the risks attached to wealth. Times are changing, however, and persons of means are beginning to come in. One purpose of his writing, therefore, is to warn the church against the dangers of secularization (riches and worldliness go hand in hand), and to remind believers of convictions about poverty and righteousness which had a noble pedigree among them.[4]

James sought in his letter to give clear instructions for how the early Jesus followers could avoid being trapped by the materialistic thinking of the world. The temptation to find personal satisfaction by gaining more material wealth and possessions would lead them to valuing possessions, or the appearance of having them, over people, which went against the foundation of trusting God that James was laying for the congregation. James was likely trying to get his readers to understand that pursuing wealth and possessions could cause a person to view others in ways contrary to how God wanted them to be seen. His readers faced the temptation of seeing other people as a means to an end instead of as colaborers for the kingdom. When that happened, God was not pleased.

James was writing to people who, as he pointed out at the beginning of the letter, had the propensity to welcome a well-dressed rich person into their congregational setting and give that rich person a place of honor over everyone else, even though that person likely became rich by taking advantage of people who were similar to those in their congregation. They looked down on others while the rich looked down on them.

For James, and God, this was unacceptable. Peck says,

Clearly there are enormous dangers in wealth. If we possess it, we must beware of it. Contrary to virtually every nuance of current North American culture, the rich are not to be thought of as persons to be mindlessly celebrated. They can lose their souls more easily than others, given what God truly values. If those who have great possessions are in the church, let them look to themselves. Let the others of us know where our trust is truly to be put.[5]

Again, James was not saying that being rich or wealthy is sinful. Rather, he's saying that we must all be aware that when we encounter wealth, we also encounter the temptation to think and behave differently. We not only see ourselves differently, but others as well.

Most readers would say, "Okay, I get James's point, but I'm not rich. I do not mistreat the poor. I have never gained an advantage over the poor. I have never made my money from laborers that were mistreated. I am not one of these rich people whom James describes." James's message is not only for the rich. It is also for those of us who may not do what the rich do yet admire them and their tactics of placing possessions over people. It is also for those of us who simply try to ignore how the poor are treated because it has nothing to do with us. Peck says, "Let everyone who has means, in the church or out of it, know that there is assuredly One who watches over the helpless, the alien, the orphan, and the mistreated toiler. There will be a reckoning in due course."[6]

In our politically charged climate, being poor has been turned into a political football for all sides of our electoral process to kick around. In the general big picture sense, those who lead our political processes choose to see the poor primarily as ammunition to attack others for their policy choices. We fail to see the poor as human beings who are as equally created in the image of God as we are. The poor retain God's light in them regardless of how they ended up in their circumstances.

We fail to see the poor as being created in God's image until we find ourselves in the same position they occupy. We often celebrate others because they have money and possessions, things many of us wish we had. We follow the rich, read their books, watch and listen to their shows, all the while hoping to learn how to be like them, forgetting that Jesus specifically said that the poor who do not have anything are closer to God than the rich who place trust in their any possessions.

As I end this chapter, I want to encourage us to begin to see the poor through the lens God employs. If the question was asked of God, "How do you see the poor?" I believe that God would respond, "I see the poor as people whom I created in love. I sent the Son as a sacrifice for their redemption, just as he was sent for yours." If God was asked the same question about the rich, I think God's response would be, "They, too, are my children, but they are no more important or more valuable than any of my other children. They are also no less important than any of my other children."

May we all adopt a perspective of faithful action that keeps God's will for our brothers and sisters close at heart. My prayer for us is that we would remember that treating the poor correctly is not a political statement but is instead a biblical mandate that comes from God. When we care for them and view them as God does, God is well pleased with us.

NOTES

1. Martin Luther King Jr., *Strive toward Freedom: The Montgomery Story* (Boston: Beacon Press, 2010), 93–94.

2. George Peck, "James 5:1–6." *Interpretation: A Journal of Bible and Theology*, 42, no. 3 (July 1988): 293.

3. Peck, 293.

4. Peck, 294.

5. Peck, 295.

6. Peck, 295.

CHAPTER 8

The Ten Commandments as a Road Map for Relationships That Honor God

How do we get back to viewing and interacting with one another in ways that honor God's image in each of us, regardless of how much we contribute to society? Is there a more ideal way for us to be in relationship with one another? Yes. I believe that God has already provided us with the road map to experience relationships that honor God's intentions for each of us. But the road map that I will suggest may not be what you anticipated when you started reading this book. I believe the most effective road map is the ten principles, or Ten Commandments, outlined in Exodus 20.

The Ten Commandments were given at a critical point in Israel's life.[1] The nation of Israel had been enslaved by a superior political and military power: the Egyptians. The Israelites were forced to live hard lives, and they consistently cried out to God for relief and freedom from their captors. Eventually, God called out to Moses, a former son of Egypt, from a burning bush and told him that God had heard the cries of God's children and that God would use him to lead them out of slavery. After a series of plagues ravaged the Egyptian people, the pharaoh granted the Israelites their freedom, allowing them to leave the land and seek out a new home for themselves, the home that had been promised to their forefather Abraham.

Life as a newly freed people was not easy for the Israelites. They did not know where they were going or how to get to their new land. In Exodus 13–17 we read stories about how the Israelites struggled as they learned what it meant to live as a freed people. They also struggled as they learned to trust God for their future. The people regularly complained about what God was asking them to do and even began to view some of the hardships they experienced as slaves in Egypt as enviable comforts when compared with the task of trusting God's leadership.

Three months into their exodus from Egypt, God stopped the people in a desert area near the foot of a mountain called Sinai. This would be the time and place where God would speak to them clearly and passionately about God's love for them and give them clear parameters for what their relationship to the Holy One, and one another, should look like. God called Moses to the top of Mount Sinai where God gave him the Ten Commandments that would dictate God's expectations for how they would live out their relationship with God and one another.

Of this important moment in Israel's life, Richard Donovan says, "This is a turning point in the life of Israel. Until now, the book of Exodus has focused on Yahweh's saving actions to bring Israel out of slavery in Egypt. Now the emphasis shifts to emphasize the covenant relationship that exists between Yahweh and Israel—and the responsibilities of Israel to Yahweh as their part of that covenant."[2] God began codifying this covenant by saying in Exodus 20:1-2 that God was the One who brought them out of Egypt and freed them from their lives of slavery. The first words of this covenant are not rules to be followed but are instead a declaration to hear, understand, and accept. That declaration is, "I am your God. I love you. I have shown my love for you by defeating your enemies and setting you free from the powers that once had control of your life." This declaration is what shapes the nine commandments that follow.

As Donovan said, this was the turning point for Israel, because just three months prior, the people had been enslaved. They had been powerless to free themselves or provide for one another. They had been dominated by an enemy who feared and loathed them. They lived where they were allowed and ate what was given to them. They gave birth to children in secret, fearing that their babies would be slaughtered. They belonged to Pharaoh. Now life was different. Now they were free in a new land. With that freedom came the need to trust God more fully for their protection, their direction in life, and their daily meals. In every sense of the word, they belonged to God and they would have to trust that God would take care of them and be true to the promises that were made to them and the generations that came before them.

The freed Israelites struggled with the idea of fully trusting God. Therefore, the first words God spoke to them at this time were critical. With the pronouncement that God was the One who freed them, God was expressing a holy devotion to these people while also expressing a desire for them to match that devotion with corresponding personal expressions of devotion to God. Everything else that God said to them through the Ten Commandments reflected the loving relationship God wanted to build with them and the future generations that would inhabit the world.

Because of this overarching desire, what followed in the remainder of Exodus 20 was not simply a list of rules or a list of dos and don'ts. It was a road map for how God's people were to live in holy relationship with God and others. The clear fulfillment of those relationships began with the fact that God was the One who, out of love, set them free together. God was not saying, "Since I have freed you, you have to do A, B, and C to stay in my good graces." Instead, God was saying, "Since I am the One who freed you, you are now able to live in a way that not only honors me but also honors self and your relationships with others."

Of this process in which God freed a people in order to fulfill relationships, Amy Erickson says,

> In the context of the larger narrative, the giving of the commandments can be understood as providing the people with a sense of purpose and identity and even a bit of security.

Although God has brought them out of Egypt and performed a number of miracles, it is not until this point in the story that God tells the people about God's intentions for them.

The commandments, however, are not simply a list of rules given to whip into shape a stiff-necked people; instead, they are better viewed as a means to form and nurture an alternative community, bound not by common goals of wealth and prestige, but rather by loyalty to a god who has chosen to redeem a group of slaves from a life of bondage. The commandments mean to sketch out a space where human beings can live fruitful, productive, and meaningful lives before God and with one another.[3]

To see the Ten Commandments as God's declaration of love and freedom for humankind is much more satisfying than carrying them around like unnecessary weight and obligation. Thomas Long challenges those who primarily see the Ten Commandments as the shortlist for staying in God's good graces by writing,

> The Decalogue begins with the good news of what the liberating God has done and then describes the shape of the freedom that results. If we want to symbolize the presence of the Ten Commandments among us, we would do well to hold a dance. The good news of the God who set people free is the music; the commandments are the dance steps of those who hear it playing. The commandments are not weights (or monuments), but wings that enable our hearts to catch the wind of God's Spirit and to soar.
>
> To see the Ten Commandments as declarations of freedom is far more satisfying than hauling around tons of dreary obligation and worrying about whether the springs and shocks are going to hold up on the flatbed truck.[4]

Through those initial words, God expressed a holy devotion to a group of people and God's desire for them to match that devotion with expressions of devotion to God. Everything else that God said to them through the Ten Commandments reflected the loving relationship God wanted to build with that group of people, the generations that would follow them, and the nations with which they would eventually interact and influence.

Understandably, Israel struggled to live into what God desired for them. They had been used to following the practices of their former slave masters, the Egyptians. Although they knew God was the ultimate God of their forefathers, they also sometimes hedged their bets by calling out to other gods. Their ongoing relationships with other gods were part of the long-term problem God had with the Hebrew people. If God did not act in a way or time frame that the Hebrews expected, they would call on other gods to fulfill their needs. In multiple Old Testament passages, God expressed displeasure and disappointment with the Hebrews for looking for help in other places.

Of this tendency to seek help in other places, Waldemar Janzen writes,

> Idolatry is the main form of covenant breaking in the Old Testament, and therefore the greatest threat to Israel's central relationship to God. Because of this tendency to look at other sources for help, God makes this the first commandment. "Don't look towards any other gods. They are not me and they will fail you. I have proven myself to you. Therefore, follow me alone."[5]

Sometimes we cannot fully understand who we are and what our relationship with others should look like because we do not have an accurate understanding of what our relationship with God is truly like. We unknowingly practice idolatry by placing our trust in a person's ability or willingness to work instead of in God's fatherly love for all humans. It is no wonder that we do not view others correctly; we do not view our connections to God correctly.

After identifying the foundation of God's relationship with humankind, God then gave, in the second commandment, a specific prohibition against the Hebrew people making idols or graven images of their Creator. Although this command seems like a no-brainer, biblical history is replete with examples of people making idols with their own hands and then worshipping those idols. This never led to anything good occurring.

When humans created images to represent God or other deities, it typically led to the people's beliefs about God being limited. Kathryn Roberts writes, "The second commandment is about limiting God. Making an image of God defines what God can or cannot be. If God is male and white, then God cannot be female and Asian. Any representation, then, is sin, because it narrows the range of possible ways God can act."[6] This tendency holds true for us today. We think that if God is primarily a God of work and action, then God's image cannot be found in those who do not work. If we can define God and what God wants according to our beliefs, then we can define the boundaries that hold God in place and the boundaries for who God can love and who can truly love God.

With the simple words of the first two commandments, "Do not worship any god except me," and "Do not make idols," God expressed a desire that the Israelites' devotion and our devotion to God would reflect God's holy devotion to God's people and that God's singular love for them and us would be reflected through a singular love for God, which would eventually lead to a broader love for others. God's desire for these words to be followed did not end in a dry desert that was inhabited by a newly freed people. God desires for us to follow these words today as if we were standing at the foot of Sinai waiting for Moses to return with two stone tablets in his hands.

But we need to remember that God's desire for us to follow this commandment and allow it to influence our view of what it means to be in relationship with God and others is not based on a selfish desire. It is based on the love that has been shown to all of us—the love that caused God to seek us when we did not want to be found, the love that caused God to save us even when we did not know we needed saving. God's commandment to give our exclusive love as an offering is simply a natural response to the love that has already been given to us. We cannot forget that the most important function of any teaching that God gave is to show us how to faithfully respond to God's grace that has already been poured out toward us.

God has the same desire for us as God had for the Hebrew people who had been freed so many years ago: God desires to be our focus. God desires that we would not put anything or anyone above Him, including a nationalistic identity. God desires that nothing else would become our "god." There is a theological and a practical reason for this, as Janzen explains:

> What is at stake in the Old Testament's fierce and persistent battle against other gods and representations of those gods formed from the stuff of the created world? The short answer is: everything that biblical faith proclaims as good news or gospel! If Israel's deliverance from Pharaoh had been accomplished by an even more powerful neighboring ruler, or by Israel's own fighting, the whole exodus story would have played itself out on the level of inner-worldly power struggle. Only by experiencing it as the leading of the Creator of the universe—a transcendent power/love, although the Old Testament does not use such abstract, philosophical terms—could Israel truly worship that God.[7]

I would add that if Israel's freedom had been achieved through sheer willpower or coordinated personal effort, then they would have believed that their future was securely in their own hands. They could rightfully place their trust in themselves and not look to God for help. And that would have likely influenced future generations, including us.

Roberts expresses the practical challenges when she says,

> We have families, jobs, and responsibilities. Acknowledging that each day we juggle competing claims on our loyalties and numerous bids for our energies may give insight into what God is saying in [these commandments]. God cannot be everything to us unless we live a cloistered life. But, in the midst of the demands on our time, our values, and our energies, YHWH

demands ultimate allegiance. There is no other to whom one owes ultimate allegiance.[8]

Not worshipping a small handmade statue is easy, but how hard is it for us to prioritize God and God's desire as it relates to the "other" as the most important activity in our lives? Judging and categorizing people based on our internal compass of self-righteous indignation is easy. It's much harder to apply the standards of grace that we believe we have received to those we think are not worthy. In learning to put God's desires first, we will have to change our personal perceptions of ourselves and others. We will have to learn that a person's worth is not derived from what they achieve but from God's unearned love.

This idea is not only found in the Old Testament. It is also regularly found in Jesus' teachings in the New Testament. The poor and foreigners held a position of great esteem in Jesus' eyes. They were not Jesus' enemies. He cherished them, regularly spent time with them, and healed them. His only regular combatants were the religious elite of the day, those who had previously held spiritual and political sway over the masses. This group regularly questioned his relationship with the poor and "other." They even questioned the validity of his ministry due to how often the "wrong" kinds of people were in Jesus' presence. Jesus ignored the complaints of the religious elite and made service to the poor and outcasts his calling card right up to the time of his death.

Why is it so hard for contemporary Christians to understand and follow Jesus' example? Because we hold others to standards that we do not hold ourselves to; we fail to recognize the grace and fortune we regularly experience in life, especially the grace found in being born within a specific period of time and within family structures that may benefit us; and we fail to see others as God sees them. These practices, whether intentional or unintentional, have helped to widen the gap between us and the people we consider unworthy of God's love or our compassion.

A New Testament passage that reiterates how to appropriately live in relationship with others is Colossians 3:12-17, which says,

God loves you and has chosen you as his own special people. So be gentle, kind, humble, meek, and patient. Put up with each other, and forgive anyone who does you wrong, just as Christ has forgiven you. Love is more important than anything else. It is what ties everything completely together.

Each one of you is part of the body of Christ, and you were chosen to live together in peace. So let the peace that comes from Christ control your thoughts. And be grateful. Let the message about Christ completely fill your lives, while you use all your wisdom to teach and instruct each other. With thankful hearts, sing psalms, hymns, and spiritual songs to God. Whatever you say or do should be done in the name of the Lord Jesus, as you give thanks to God the Father because of him.

Here Paul showed us the heart of what the Ten Commandments was pointing toward: Love toward all people should be a daily commitment that we all adopt.

The letter to the church in Colossae was written by Paul during one of his times of imprisonment. He wrote it to the church in the region, which was a minor city located about a hundred miles east of Ephesus. The city had previously been a thriving place of commerce, but due to multiple factors, it eventually lost its affluence and notoriety. Paul wrote the letter to remind his readers of what should be important to them. He stressed that nothing could, or should, come before their commitment to Christ and his teachings. Christ is preeminent in all things. He is greater than all earthly things, and the sacrifice he made for their salvation is complete and wholly sufficient.

Paul also wrote to the Colossians to refute an erroneous way of thinking and practicing faith that had begun to creep into their services. It stressed a low view of the body, the importance of circumcision, dietary regulations, ritual observance, worship of angels, and preoccupation with mystical experiences. It was extremely legalistic and focused on doing certain things to prove one's high level of spirituality. In this new way of thinking, the best way to prove that you were righteous was to perform certain legalistic deeds.

Paul spent considerable time in the letter telling his readers what they should not do and what they should get rid of in their lives. He told them to put to death certain habits, to rid themselves of certain beliefs, and to take off certain practices and set them aside, never to pick them up again. He warned them against being fooled by false teachers. Do not be cheated by people who have a false sense of humility. Do not be tricked into following a set of rules, hoping to find salvation in them. Christ had freed them from having to follow those types of things and from being under a load of guilt for not following a prescribed set of unnecessary guidelines.

Paul wanted to reassure them that the system of thinking that was creeping into their community was insufficient for their salvation and the fruits that this system of thinking produced were not the kinds of fruit God was looking for. The kind of fruit that God wanted to see from them was not legalism but love. God wanted them to have a new mindset that led to new practices within their local community as well as the broader community. They were to make love their foundation because it was the foundation through which God had been gentle, kind, and patient with them. Because of God's foundation of love, they had been forgiven and restored to the right relationship with God through Christ.

The love that they were to exhibit in their lives was not just to be a sometimes love that was to be exhibited only when they felt like it or when someone agreed with them. This practice of love was to be so encompassing that it covered them like clothing. In a few short verses, Paul transitioned from saying, "Get rid of this and do not do that," to saying, "Wear love like a garment. Develop a new practice! Make love your focus." Amy Peeler says it this way:

> As ones God has chosen, set apart as holy and loved, they should make sure their behavior matches up with their identity; their outside should match their inside. Knowing who they are helps them to clothe themselves with behavior that fits. Just as ill-fitting clothes detract from the beauty of a person, so too

do ill-fitting behaviors detract from the image of Christ that believers should exhibit.[9]

Paul continued this line of thinking in verses 15-17 of Colossians 3 while also showing that this idea was much bigger than one single person. They all may have had individual responsibilities to exhibit the qualities of Christ, but they could not do that in personal vacuums. The entire body would have to face this challenge together. This foundational idea of love and how it is lived out within community was not just for the benefit of one person but for the benefit of the entire community. I appreciate Marion Soards's commentary on these verses. He says,

> Whatever actions the Christians take are taken because of what God has done—that is, Christian life is the consequence of the gospel. . . . Christians are to "put on" certain characteristics so that they live these qualities, they do not merely "have" them. Not merely traits, but actions define Christian living. As Christ lived, so the Christians are to live. . . . Thus, that which the community experiences, the community is called to live out— and here, it is crucial to see that the "you"s of these verses are consistently in plural forms; that is, the author addresses the community, not merely the pious individual. . . . The gospel is personal, but it is not—based upon these verses—to be made private. The text of Colossians envisions a community in action.[10]

This message of love found in Christ is not a message that is too heavy or burdensome, either. It's something that Paul's readers were to find comfort and joy in. This new way of thinking and acting was something to be celebrated and rejoiced over. It was not to be viewed as a chore or an inconvenience. It was to be bought into wholeheartedly because God bought into it wholeheartedly for all of them, and for us, through Christ.

As was true for Paul's original audience, love was one of the primary things, if not the primary thing, that we should be focusing on, and not just within our organized religious life, but within our personal lives, as well. It is the ideal that should lead our words, actions, and beliefs in life. It should be the thing that we practice consistently from day to day. It should be the foundation of each new year that we are privileged to enter. It should be our focus because God made it his focus on our behalf.

In Paul's words, we find the cure for a culture that has progressively become more secluded and distant from one another and less compassionate with every passing day. He gives a clear explanation of what God hopes that we would all do daily: Love others as we have been loved, regardless of political affiliation. Show compassion to others, especially those we consider unlovable, as it has been shown to us. Treat others like we would want to be treated, even when we do not feel like it. In doing this, the world will see Christ reflected not just in our words but in our actions, and they will know they can be in relationship with God and us. If we can figure out how to do this on a regular basis, God will be glorified, and that is the point of all of this anyway.

As we replace bootstrap theology with a gospel of generosity and justice, we begin to understand that the value people hold before God is not based on how much they produce in society, how often they work, or how long they are able to maintain a job, but is instead based on the love that God inherently has for all creation. We then begin to have a more faithful view of God and one another and are able to develop steps to more appropriately live in relationship with one another.

NOTES

1. Michael Coogan, *The Ten Commandments: A Short History of an Ancient Text* (New Haven, CT: Yale University Press, 2014).

2. Richard Donovan, "Biblical Commentary Exodus 20:1-20," Sermon Writer, accessed May 10, 2019, https://sermonwriter.com/biblical-commentary/old-testament-exodus-201-20-commentary/.

3. Amy Erickson, "Commentary on Exodus 20:1-4, 7-9, 12-20," Working Preacher, October 2, 2011, https://www.workingpreacher.org/preaching.aspx?commentary_id=1068.

4. Thomas Long, "Dancing the Decalogue," Living by the Word, March 7, 2006, https://www.christiancentury.org/article/2006-03/dancing-decalogue.

5. Waldemar Janzen, "The First Commandments of the Decalogue and the Battle against Idolatry in the Old Testament," *Vision* 12, no. 1 (2011): 15.

6. Kathryn L. Roberts, "Between Text & Sermon: Exodus 20:1-6," *Interpretation* Vol. No 61, Issue No 1. (2007): 62.

7. Janzen, "The First Commandments of the Decalogue," 15.

8. Roberts, "Between Text & Sermon," 62.

9. Amy Peeler, "Commentary on Colossians 3:12-17," Working Preacher, December 30, 2012, https://www.workingpreacher.org/preaching.aspx?commentary_id=1506.

10. Marion Soards, "Commentary on Colossians 3:12-17," Working Preacher, December 27, 2009, https://www.workingpreacher.org/preaching.aspx?commentary_id=482.

CHAPTER 9

A Community of Inclusion, Equality, and Hope

The *Peanuts* comic strip was created by Charles Schulz in 1947 as a weekly strip for Schulz's hometown newspaper, the *St. Paul Pioneer Press*.[1] Within three years of its inclusion in the paper, the strip grew in popularity and circulation, eventually being picked up by a syndicate, which led to *Peanuts* being published in 2,600 newspapers, with a readership of around 355 million across seventy-five countries with translation into twenty-one languages. As a budding cartoonist in high school, I was just happy to be the staff cartoonist for my high school newspaper.

In total, *Peanuts* ran from 1947 to 2000, and Mr. Schulz drew 17,897 strips.[2] The longevity of the strip was based on the unique intersection of the characters, who were all elementary school–aged children, and the clearly adult subject matter they regularly discussed. No subject matter was off-limits for Charlie Brown, Linus, Lucy, Snoopy, or the rest of their crew. For example, *Peanuts* was one of the first comic strips to show black and white children as friends and classmates. The characters talked about war and its effects on them and their families. They talked about politics. They even talked about God and whether they felt God was paying attention to them.

But their favorite subject matter was always their relationships, whether it was the strip's main character, Charlie Brown, expressing his desire to be in a relationship with the cute red-headed girl; Lucy sitting at her psychiatrist stand doling out psychological advice for five cents; or Sally needing advice because she had a crush on Schroeder, the piano virtuoso, and wanted him to fall in love with her instead of his stupid piano.

One of the characters who struggled with relationships the most was Lucy's younger brother, Linus. Most times, Linus felt more comfortable with a blanket than he did with people. Linus had keen insight into how people treated one another, and it influenced his perception of them. This was especially seen in the interactions between Linus and his sister, Lucy, in a particular strip. In it, Linus opined, "I love humanity. It's the people I can't stand." Have you ever felt like that before? Truthfully, I have felt like that often. I've felt that way not because I do not like people in general but because people can sometimes make themselves unlikable.

The words expressed by Linus in that strip eventually spawned a new philosophical term, *Schulz's paradox*,[3] which sought to understand whether it is possible to love all humankind while not liking people as individuals. The question the paradox raises is whether a person can truly love humanity without loving every individual human. Can you truly be part of a community without loving the other members of that community? I do not think this paradox or the question it raises are new. I think we find elements of this paradox, the challenge of loving humanity and loving individuals, throughout the Bible, including in the Ten Commandments and Jesus' teachings related to them.

During the days when the events of the Hebrew Bible were occurring, there were multiple ways that a person was understood to be acceptable within a community. The primary way was based on a person's willingness to follow the communal religious principles God set forth for everyone to follow: Worship God alone. Do not make any false idols to place your trust in. Do not use God's name in vain. Take time to rest, as God did. Honor your relationships with those who raised and positively influenced you. Treat others in respectful ways by not stealing from them or wanting what is theirs, including their spouses. And honor God's image in other people.

These acts of kindness were not only to be practiced toward people who were a part of one's tribe. They were to be shown to anyone with whom a person came in contact who was not a stated enemy of God or God's plans. That meant that God's followers were to show the same concern and respect for people who were not like them. They were to honor God's image found in strangers and foreigners. Why were they to do this? Because God's children had once been foreigners in a strange land, and they could remember what it felt like to be treated as less than human.

Jesus and his followers taught and lived by these principles, as well, although the process of welcoming people who were different from them was not always easy. Jesus' ministry was built on practicing kindness to those who were considered as "other"—so much so that he was regularly challenged by the religious leaders of his day for having unacceptable people in his entourage. As the early church grew, multiple conversations occurred about who was and who was not going to be allowed to participate in God's family. Eventually, the disciples understood that the requirements they believed were necessary for someone to participate in God's kingdom were not accurate and that God's family would probably be bigger than they anticipated.

It took the early church time to begin to recognize that God was doing something different in the world through them. Although God was not getting rid of the many laws and principles that had served as the bedrock of prior generations, God was trying to show them that those laws and principles were being fulfilled through Jesus and the things he had been teaching his followers. The ability or willingness to follow a set of rules was not the primary identifying marker for members of God's family. God wasn't most concerned about a person's ability to live according to a set of rules or communal expectations. Instead, a willingness to see people as God saw them—of inherent value because they were created in God's image—and treating them as God would, would become the sign that someone was a part of God's family.

This process of rethinking what it meant to be a part of God's family was difficult for the early church and caused division among leaders and families. Relationships were strained and broken. Multiple meetings and conversations were held. But in the end, the church realized that they had to rethink everything they had once held as important. We have this same opportunity today. We no longer need to view people and their value within society through the lens of bootstrap theology, which does not take into account how the world has changed and how systems have been used to keep certain people "in their place," and fails to recognize the inherent value all people possess. Instead of using the belief that persons have to earn their keep to be pleasing to God and others as our guide for interacting with others, following Jesus' example of welcoming and affirming anyone who earnestly seeks to understand their relationship with God should be our primary criteria.

As Jesus taught in the vineyard parable found in Matthew 20:1-16, God is less concerned about how long or how much a person works. Instead, God cares first about a person's willingness to hear God calling them and inviting them to participate in building God's kingdom. Matthew 20:1-16 is a parable about a landowner (who in most interpretations represents God) and his dealings with those he has hired to work on his farm (most interpretations say those workers represent us).[4]

The landowner went out searching for laborers to work in his vineyard at five separate times on the same day. He hired workers in the wee hours of the morning, at 9:00 a.m., 12:00 p.m., 3:00 p.m., and 5:00 p.m. Each time the landowner talked with a group of laborers, he agreed to pay them a reasonable wage for their work, and each group agreed to the landowner's terms and went to work. At the end of the day, things did not turn out as everyone had anticipated. Everyone was paid the same wage—that is, those who worked two hours got paid the same as those who worked ten hours.

Not all the workers thought it was fair, and they were not happy with how the day ended, while others were overjoyed with how the day turned out for them. The owner's response to the workers' frustration was interesting, to say the least. He essentially told them that he had paid them all a fair wage. He paid them what was agreed upon. No more and no less. What gave them the right to be frustrated in response to his generosity to their fellow workers? Kathryn Blanchard comments,

> Hard-working good people have always asked: what kind of God would offer the same reward to those who have earned it and those who have not? This parable makes clear that there is radical equality before God. Reward comes not from each worker's individual merit, not from the quantity or even quality of their labor, but rather from the gracious covenant offered by the one doing the hiring. God promises and delivers but one reward for all—enough for one's daily bread.[5]

This parable seems to be about fair wages for honest labor, but is this parable just about money? Is it just about wages earned for the time put in, or is there more to it than that? Charles Campbell has this to say:

> Their complaint does not simply concern money; it goes much deeper, to what the money represents. The real issue is superiority: "you have made them equal to us." Work becomes not simply the means for earning daily bread, but a source of division and competition, a means of reinforcing the categories of winners and losers, superior and inferior.[6]

The parable is not just about defining a fair wage for a fair day's work. Charlotte Cleghorn writes, "It goes against our sensibilities of what is just and fair, and this is a danger for any of us hearing the parables and trying to make sense of them as twenty-first-century Christians."[7] Cleghorn continues,

> This parable is essentially about the generosity of God. It is not about equity or proper disbursement of wages but about a gracious and undeserved gift. It is not about an economic exchange but, rather, about a bestowing of grace and mercy to

all, no matter what time they have put in or how deserving or undeserving we may think them to be. God's generosity often violates our own sense of right and wrong, our sense of how things would be if we ran the world.[8]

In other words, "God extends benevolence to everyone, regardless of what they may have earned by worldly standards, so those already called by God should exemplify piety and exhort others to live humbly in service to God rather than mumble about inequitable treatment."[9]

I do not believe that a person is free from participating in tangible efforts to provide for themselves. I do believe that if a person is able to work and make a positive contribution to society, then they are obligated to do so. I understand, and in a sense agree with the idea, that if a person wants to receive the benefits that come from being a part of a community, they should make some effort to fulfill at least some of the requirements the community holds participants to, including working and earning an honest day's wages. As Michael Turner writes, "The individual's responsibility is to maximize the gifts God has provided and to recognize that whatever good comes from personal effort is ultimately attributable to God."[10]

But we cannot forget that not everyone in our society is offered the same rights and opportunities as others simply because of the color of their skin, their place of origin, and their gender. Our society has made this amply evident through our history of racism, sexism, and classism. We tend either to forget this fact or to fail to acknowledge its reality when we attempt to hold certain people and groups to a standard that fails to consider their lived experiences. We do not think about how they have personally and corporately been treated unfairly so others like us can achieve or excel. Or we forget that sometimes life happens to others in ways that are unfamiliar to us, yet we believe they should be able to overcome since someone else overcame a life experience we see as similar to theirs.

We also cannot forget that God's image is found in everyone. The idea that we should first seek to find God's image in all people is not unique to the Old Testament. In multiple places, Jesus took up this idea and shared it in new ways with his followers. One of those occasions was in Luke 4:14-21.

After Jesus was baptized by John in the Jordan, confirmed as God's chosen messenger through the descending of the Holy Spirit, and subsequently spent forty days in the wilderness where he overcame the temptation to trust in his own power, Jesus burst onto the religious scene with words that rivaled those delivered by Moses to a hopeless people generations before. He said, "I have good news for those who need it. The time has come. Your freedom has arrived." Like the prophets of old, Jesus was saying that debts were going to be expunged, sin would be forgiven, people would be set free, hope would be restored, and dreams of a brighter day would come true. Jesus' proclamation was akin to saying to get ready, for something that looked like it was dying would instead be reborn.

Jesus' coming and the words he shared that day signaled a rebirth for God's people. As their ancestors waited for a new day to dawn for them, Jesus was saying that a new day was dawning for those who were listening to him and those who would witness his ministry. Just as their Hebrew ancestors had held on to dreams and promises handed down by past generations that they would one day be saved by God from Egyptian oppression and become a great nation that would be in unbroken relationship with God, on that day, Jesus was affirming the same thing for his listeners.

The words Jesus read from the Isaiah scrolls described the Messiah who was to come and save and free God's people, restore broken relationships, and give hope to the hopeless. He told them that he was the embodiment of what they had prayed for and dreamed about. Jesus' announcement acknowledged how things had been but also foretold what things would eventually be like. The overlooked and forgotten would be restored to their rightful places.

I have heard someone describe God's words about making life better for the Hebrews, and in turn, making life better for the nations they would meet, and Jesus' words in Luke 4 as words of eschatological hope.[11] His words did not signify the end of life or the world. Instead, they signaled the end of hopelessness and the beginning of new life. They represented rebirth, new opportunity, and new hope. Hope that was not far off in the distance but could be experienced in the here and now. And that hope was not only for one group of people. It was for everyone. Jesus' listeners could believe that their lives, and the lives of others, could be changed for the better as they listened to and followed Jesus.

Jesus' words and ministry were not only spiritual; they were moral and practical, as well. Jesus' life was spent not only making a spiritual difference in people's lives but making a tangible difference in people's immediate circumstances. This opportunity to make a tangible difference, this immediacy in helping others, is the example we are to follow today. I would even say that as followers of Christ and believers in God's love, we are required to follow in Christ's footsteps in helping others. We cannot do what Jesus did to proclaim hope to the hopeless without being led by the same Spirit that led him to share the words found in Luke 4. We cannot be led by a spirit of separation or exclusion based on race, gender, or economic standing.

We must be led by the Spirit that descended upon Jesus at his baptism, empowered him to set aside personal safety, and encouraged him to fulfill his calling to restore relationships between God and humans. This same Spirit kept him from viewing people who were different from him or who had different life circumstances from him as "other." This same Spirit that caused him to become the hands and feet of God in tangible ways is the same Spirit who seeks to empower all of us to regularly imitate Jesus' words, actions, and attitudes. The Spirit is just waiting for us to make ourselves available.

Ultimately, our eternal hope is not found in taking sides against those who are different from us. Our hope is partially found in our willingness to live into the message that Jesus declared in that synagogue. We all have hope because God loves us and is actively seeking to be in relationship with each of us, regardless of our life situation. And God wants us to figure out how to be in relationship with others too. Our priorities should not be our possessions or how possessions affect our lives. Instead, they should be how our attitudes affect our relationships with others. This was a consistent part of Jesus' message during his ministry.

As we have seen through the commandments of Exodus 20, God gives to people, no matter how big or small that gift may be, for those who receive to be able to give to others as they have been blessed. God wanted the original hearers of the words in Exodus to understand that they did not live in a vacuum or live for their own fulfillment. They lived as part of a larger whole. The possessions God allowed them to have were not simply for their own enjoyment but also for the betterment of the whole community.

The Hebrew people understood the idea of owning something in two primary ways. First, possessions were made possible by God's actions of providing those possessions. Anything that a person owned came directly from God or through God's providential action. Anything that they would be able to claim as their own would come from God providing it for them. Since the Hebrew people were a tightly knit community, each person had the opportunity to produce something that benefited others, and everyone had the opportunity to receive the benefits of something someone else had produced. The possessions God gave were not to be kept or hoarded for the use of only one person. They were to benefit the entire body.

In essence, we are blessed by God to bless others. This attitude is the calling card for those who inhabit God's kingdom. We violate God's principles every time we engage in practices that keep people from experiencing biblical community based on their ability or willingness to work, or that exclude them based on their race or country of origin.

This attitude is the fulfillment of the paradox of Christian life in community. Jesus taught his followers that loving others would require that they not hold others to an unrealistic standard. We face the same challenges as Jesus' original followers faced. How do we navigate the challenges that come with being humans who are trying to do life together with other humans? How do we respond when other humans do not live up to the standards we think they should? R. C. Sproul once said, "When we are honest with ourselves, some Christians are easier to love than others. We all find certain people less offensive than others, and as a result, we will gravitate toward those we consider lovable. But Christ does not call us to love only those easy to love. After all, He Himself died for sinners."[12]

Sometimes we spend too much time identifying the sins of others and forget that we are fallible ourselves and often fail to get things right. How should other people respond when we do not live in the faith that we have been called to? In his book *Everyday Ethics: Inspired Solutions to Real-Life Dilemmas*, Joshua Halberstam amplifies Linus's words, "I love humanity. It's the people I can't stand" to provide sage insight into people who claim to be the loving people God calls them to be yet fail to live into God's desires for how others are to be treated. "In general, the devotion to humanity is often a mask for an inability to connect to other people on a personal level. Some of the greatest 'lovers of mankind' have downright ugly histories when it comes to their personal relationships."[13] Halberstam goes on to ask why this matters. His answer: "Our emotions are directed to individuals, not abstractions."[14] This paradox is not simply a theory. It is a reality that we all are living in today.

So being a loving person is less about what you say and more about what you do in concrete ways. The best way to show that you are living in God's call to live out of God's abundance of light instead of the limited darkness is to be intentional within every single relationship in which you find yourself. Since Jesus gave us the ultimate example of living in ways that please God and honor others, we who claim to follow him should do all that we can to live in ways that honor him and those with whom we are in community.

NOTES

1. Charles M. Schulz, *Peanuts: A Golden Celebration. The Art and the Story of the World's Best-Loved Comic Strip* (New York: Harper-Collins, 2004).

2. Charles M. Schulz.

3. David Langness, "I Love Mankind—It's People I Can't Stand!" May 30, 2017, BahaiTeachings.org.

4. Stanley Hauerwas, *Matthew* (Grand Rapids: Brazos, 2007).

5. Kathryn Blanchard, "Theological Perspective on Matthew 20:1-16," in *Feasting on the Word: Year A*, David L. Bartlett and Barbara Brown Taylor, gen. eds. (Louisville: Westminster John Knox, 2010), 4:94.

6. Charles Campbell, "Homiletical Perspective on Matthew 20:1-16," in *Feasting on the Word: Year A*, David L. Bartlett and Barbara Brown Taylor, gen. eds. (Louisville: Westminster John Knox, 2010), 4:97.

7. Charlotte Cleghorn, "Pastoral Perspective on Matthew 20:1-16," in *Feasting on the Word: Year A*, David L. Bartlett and Barbara Brown Taylor, gen. eds. (Louisville: Westminster John Knox, 2010), 4:92.

8. Cleghorn, 96.

9. Michael Turner, "Retrieving the Moral Significance of Deserving for Protestant Ethics: Calvin's Commentaries on Personal Desert in Economic Exchange," *Journal of the Society of Christian Ethics* 34, no. 2 (2014): 132.

10. Turner, 135.

11. John T. Squires, "Acts," *Eerdmans Commentary on the Bible*, ed. James Dunn and John William Rogerson (Grand Rapids: Eerdmans, 2003).

12. Robert Charles Sproul, "Love Your Brothers," Ligonier Ministries, accessed October 26, 2019, https://www.ligonier.org/learn/devotionals/love-your-brothers/.

13. Joshua Halberstam, *Everyday Ethics: Inspired Solutions to Real-Life Dilemmas* (New York: Penguin, 1994), 178.

14. Halberstam, 178.

Conclusion

The *Phantom of the Opera* was written by the successful French crime novelist Gaston Leroux and first appeared in novel form in 1910.[1] Although Leroux was already an established fiction writer by the time of the novel's publication, his reputation was further cemented through *Phantom of the Opera*. The novel was successfully interpreted in movie form multiple times before Andrew Lloyd Webber reenvisioned it as a musical in 1986. Lloyd Webber's vision has proven to be one of the most enduring and celebrated productions in the history of Broadway.

At its core, the *Phantom of the Opera* is about love. Needed and hoped-for love. Requited and unrequited love. This requited and unrequited love are best understood through the lives and relationships of the story's three main characters: Erik, Christine, and Raoul.

Erik is the Phantom. Because he was born with a physical deformity, he has not experienced personal love or love from a community. He was described at birth as appearing corpse-like and looking like a living skull. Since I am a 1980s baby, I imagine he looked like a version of Skeletor from the *He-Man* cartoon series. In subsequent movies and the musical, his deformity covers half his face, making him look like a circus show freak. Erik missed out on love because everyone was repulsed by his looks, even his mother.

In the novel, Erik makes up for unexperienced love by traveling to foreign lands as a circus performer and builder of trick palaces. He also learns construction and engineering, and from his well-rounded experiences, he begins to create physical and musical masterpieces that find their culmination in the bowels of a Parisian opera house. While living below the opera house, Erik finds love in the voice of a young soprano named Christine. He is enraptured with her talent and looks but knows that she would be repulsed by his appearance. So he forms a relationship with her by whispering compliments and advice through the walls of her dressing room.

Christine is a young singer who is just hoping for an opportunity to show the world how much she loves singing opera, but she has been overlooked as a viable singer and surpassed by others not as talented as she. Although she does not receive love from those who run the opera house, she finds the compliments and attention she craves from the angelic voice behind the walls of her dressing room. The voice of the "Angel of the Opera" affirms her talents and dreams. Over time she begins to feel love for this angel, but how could she fall in love with someone she has never actually seen in person?

As fate would have it, a long-forgotten friend reappears in Christine's life, giving her a glimpse of what true love could look like. That friend is Raoul, whom she has not seen since her childhood. Christine has never seen Raoul as anything but a friend, but Raoul has nurtured a crush on Christine since they were children. But they are no longer children. She is a blossoming opera star, and he is now a handsome and successful man. As an adult, he now has the opportunity to finally be with this woman whom he has loved for so long. He eventually proposes, she accepts, and everyone is happy. Well, everyone except the angelic voice behind the dressing room walls. In jealousy and anger, a deformed version of love, the Phantom of the Opera sets a plan in motion to destroy Christine, Raoul, and the opera. If he cannot have her, no one will.

Erik wanted love from his family and community, but his deformity made him unlovable. The love he was able to experience through his relationship with Christine was deformed because that love was based on jealousy and a need to control. Christine wanted love from her community, but it was elusive because other people overlooked her talents. Raoul wanted love from Christine, and he was willing to wait to receive it. Have you experienced love in any of these ways?

Although love was prominent in the story of the Phantom of the Opera, the love displayed was not always healthy—kind of like the love people say they have when they challenge the "other" to work for what they have or to be more patriotic or to learn to speak English since they are in America. This type of love is based on a deformed idea of love for a country instead of love for people, which puts the ideal first and the person a distant second.

The Bible enables us to address these various types of deformed ideals of love by teaching us the skills necessary to navigate the challenges that come with being in relationship with people who buy into deformed ideals of love. The Bible teaches us what healthy love looks like. Healthy love looks drastically different from unhealthy love, and healthy love has positive effects on individuals and communities while the effects of unhealthy love are detrimental to both.

Healthy love is patient with others, acts kindly toward others, is not jealous of others, does not brag on itself, is not proud of itself, does not act in inappropriate ways toward others, does not desire things for itself above things that would benefit others, and does not easily get upset with others. Instead, healthy love rejoices when other people rejoice, is willing to help others bear their burdens, believes in others, hopes on behalf of others, and endures the trials and tribulations that come with being in relationship with others without keeping score of how many times someone has done them wrong (1 Corinthians 13:4-8).

Love, the kind that God wants for God's children and the kind demonstrated by the sacrifice of Jesus, is sacrificial and accommodating of the needs of others. It understands that sometimes people will not rise to their full potential and does not hold that against them. Instead, it comforts them and supports them and seeks to find ways to remind them that God still loves them. Unfortunately, bootstrap theology struggles with this idea. The characters in the *Phantom of the Opera* also struggled with it.

Erik's understanding of love was fractured because his mother and the communities he previously occupied failed to show him the healthy love he needed and craved. This left a tremendous void in his life that he tried to fill with Christine. Unfortunately, his love for Christine was based on a desire to control her and make up for something that was missing from his own life experience. Christine's understanding of love was also fractured because she was seeking the approval of others in an opera community that had not yet accepted her and failed to recognize the gifts she wanted to bring to the community. She filled that gap with the unhealthy attention Erik gave her. Ultimately, all this unhealthy love led to the near-death of Raoul, the one person who seemed to love Christine with a sincere love. Raoul's love was not necessarily sacrificial, but it was true. As Christine began to better understand Raoul's love for her, her love for him transformed to a sacrificial love that fought to keep him alive. But in the end, no one really won.

Although I know *Phantom of the Opera* is a fictional piece, I cannot help but think how the characters and their lives would have turned out differently if their communities would have loved them adequately. If Erik's mother and the people he came in contact with had looked past his external scars to see the creativity in his heart, he likely would have used all the skills and talents he developed during his travels to create meaningful art and architecture instead of plotting to harm others. If Christine's community had loved her and recognized her talents, she likely would not have had to look for acceptance from a strange voice behind a wall. And ultimately, people's lives would not have been changed so drastically.

The necessity for us to love others with a godly love is one of the primary subjects the church needs to address in the twenty-first century: How should we view and interact with anyone whom we consider "other" because their lives do not rise to our standards? Will room be made for them in God's kingdom if they do not get their lives together? What is our relationship with them to look like if we are positively contributing to God's kingdom through our work and they are not making any significant impact?

Is God's love for those types of people as significant as God's love for us? Why would God consider allowing people like that into the kingdom in the first place? If a person is a sinner, which is the designation we are giving them, are they worthy of redemption?

How many lives in our communities are affected like Erik's and Christine's? How many times have we looked at people's scars (the things we deem are unacceptable and that they should fix to be found acceptable by us) first instead of looking into their hearts? How many times have we missed opportunities to recognize and support others? How often have we missed opportunities to love others as we have been loved? How could a new, or renewed, understanding and practice of loving others, no matter how different they are from us, affect the communities we live in?

In light of all that continues to occur in our world, country, and communities, I pray that we continue to think about love's implications in our lives and the lives of others and actively seek out opportunities to put Jesus' principles of love, regardless of external factors, into practice.

NOTES

1. Gaston Leroux, *Phantom of the Opera* (n.p.: Pierre Lafitte, 1909).

Index

REFLECTIVE
Study Guide

This Reflective Study Guide for *Taking Apart Bootstrap Theology: Gospel of Generosity and Justice* provides an additional opportunity for individuals and groups to reflect and show how racism and class affect people's work and lives. For example, the push for individualism by white evangelicals and a bootstrap theology is at the expense of minorities and the poor. In this Reflective Study Guide, this issue and more are explored.

Taking apart bootstrap theology requires a willingness to change and do things differently. Thoughts and feelings rooted in supporting the power structure, a select racial group, and the belief that each person is responsible for his or her destiny cannot continue to be the norm of a society, nation, and individuals.

Dismantling a bootstrap theology requires Christians to accept God as the foundation for strengthening and guiding persons to love, care, and treat others as God's created beings. God's expectation of generosity and justice is the framework from which evangelicalism can build and maintain healthy and life-giving opportunities to emerge and thrive.

Each section of this Reflective Study Guide is based on the chapters in this book and anecdotal pieces. Participants will have chances to respond to the questions based on their experiences. There is blank space for you to write your thoughts and feelings on a selected statement. You can use this space to express yourself by writing a prayer, poem, one word, or a drawing related to the subject. Additional pages for writing notes are at the end of the Reflective Study Guide.

Preface

Assumptions can provide a good or bad thought about someone. Images and feelings are associated with either of these feelings. If repeated enough, sometimes the person they are about think they are true. These false truisms lead people to construct a reality that becomes a "natural" part of life and laws that everyone must follow.

1. Various family members and neighbors often play a critical role in raising children and grandchildren within their families. Identify three persons who impacted your childhood through your teen years. Identify two ways they helped shape who you are today and challenged you to move beyond negative beliefs that people had about you or your race.

2. What assumptions have others made about you that either encouraged or hurt you? How did these assumptions make you feel, and what was your response then and now?

3. Share what you would say to encourage a thirteen-year-old individual based on what you now know about the world today and the beliefs or assumptions said to you when growing up.

REFLECTION SPACE

Write or express your thoughts or feelings about why knowing who you are in the Lord is necessary despite what society or others say about you.

Part One:
Exploring Bootstrap Theology

A. An Introduction to Bootstrap Theology

1. Explain why you agree or disagree with the definition of bootstrap theology.

2. One of the tenets identified in bootstrap theology is that your status in life is equated with a person's job. Is this a reality that is perpetuated, and is it lived out in the church as well?

3. Identify two bootstrap theology purposes within the introduction that remain hindrances to creating a more just community? Explain.

REFLECTION SPACE

Write or express your thoughts or feelings about why political, religious, and economic systems continue to support racial injustices.

B. The Foundations of Bootstrap Theology

1. Reread 2 Thessalonians 3:6-13. Paul advocates for persons to work and not become idle waiting for Jesus to return. Why is idleness a threat to the teachings of Christ, as Paul states? What keeps some people, as the Thessalonians did, from moving forward and allowing others to take care of them?

2. Bootstrap Theology is legitimized by white evangelical Christians and others because God laid the foundation for work and supplied additional creation resources. Share an example of how bootstrap theology was used against someone in your family or friends.

3. Calvin built upon Luther's strong work ethic. Both agreed that work was necessary. Their beliefs helped to form a strong Protestant work ethic that continues today. What are the benefits of a strong work ethic? Calvin placed values on types of labor, which influenced a person's class or status. Identify aspects of how classism operates for job choices within your community and family.

REFLECTION SPACE

Write or express your thoughts or feelings regarding an excerpt by Kathryn Blanchard on Calvin's belief that "most economic decisions, therefore, were by and large matters of individual conscience as long as they did not offend God's laws" (Kathryn Blanchard, *The Protestant Ethic or the Spirit of Capitalism: Christians, Freedom, and Free Markets*).

C. The Problems with Bootstrap Theology

1. Individualism is a bootstrap theology problem because it promotes that individuals have full control of their work choices. Based on the analysis provided about evangelism's perspectives on individualism, share an example of how various faith communities support individuality without examining structures or systems that work against an individual trying to find work.

2. Decision-makers have significant input and control over another person's ability to work. Identify two options to help evangelical Christians who believe a person's ability to work or not is only because of choices made by an individual.

3. Jesus cared for the poor and challenged the systems that left the poor marginalized and poverty-stricken. Why are evangelicals and others resistant to providing for the poor and eradicating poverty?

REFLECTION SPACE

Write or express your thoughts or feelings by stating the pros and cons of evangelicalism's focus on a personal relationship with Christ through various spiritual practices. Note Emerson and Smith's perspective on evangelicalism individualism and a personal relationship with Christ in the section, "The Problems with Bootstrap Theology."

Part Two:
Dismantling Bootstrap Theology

A. End Nationalistic Christianity

1. Nationalistic Christianity serves for the benefit of whom? Provide three examples of groups and individuals who have and are benefitting from a nationalistic Christianity.

2. The Indigenous people of the United States were massacred, their land was stolen, and they were forced to live on "reservations." How should the nation and other racial groups work to change the wrong done to Native people?

3. Bootstrap theology holds individuals responsible for their inability to work and life circumstances. Write a short story that speaks to the responsible persons who have individually and collectively helped to care for and promote justice for one another.

REFLECTION SPACE

Write or express your thoughts or feelings that humanity is made in the image of God. If all people are made in the image of God, the *imago Dei*, Genesis 1:27, give reasons as to why some Christians place higher values on particular people more than others. Are you a person who places a higher value on some people more than you do others? Why?

B. Change the Perspective on Race and Crime

1. Identify how race is used against persons who are arrested for committing crimes. In your community, are there organizations or groups who develop or collaborate for changes in the criminal justice system or provide resources for persons and their families who are released from incarceration?

2. Review the exclusion reasons that poor people and poverty continue to remain significant problems in the United States. Why are Jesus' words, "The poor will be with you always," (Matthew 26:11) relevant now? Share how bootstrap theology supports maintaining poverty economically and in people's spirits.

3. What are two practices the author lists to dismantle bootstrap theology? Add at least one more item that the author does not include and state why.

REFLECTION SPACE

Write or express your thoughts or feelings about churches that do well at providing food baskets, clothing, prayer, moral support, sick visitation, prison visits, and more. Plan a church strategy with various church ministries and community groups or join one to contact politicians, wealthy companies, and individuals to end poverty or address at least one issue that exists because of poverty.

C. Expand the Perception of
Who Is Worthy of God's Love

1. If minorities are considered unclean, what is the Christian choice and lifestyle to changing this belief? According to some Christians, if we are all sinners, why are some sinners less loved by God?

2. Select a parable from Luke 15 and apply it to how your relationship motivates you to help others connect to the love of Christ regardless of their circumstances.

3. Bootstrap theology keeps us from accepting that God's love is for all. In what contexts have you experience persons denying you love or acceptance or from a worldwide perspective? Who helped you to know and feel love again or work through your pain?

REFLECTION SPACE

Write or express your thoughts or feelings regarding when you have wanted God not to show love or bless someone. Elaborate on your emotions and reasons for wanting God to act like that. Have you asked God for forgiveness or changed your behavior inwardly or outwardly toward the person?

Part Three:
Replacing Bootstrap Theology with a Gospel of Generosity and Justice

A. A Biblically Faithful View of Wealth and Poverty

1. The Bible does not say that persons cannot be wealthy, but it strongly opposes rich people not helping someone they can help. Read James 5:1-6. Discuss with a colleague or friend about the parallel with verses 4-6 in contemporary times.

2. We live in a competitive society. Labels of winners and losers, superior and inferior, are commonplace. Are these labels necessary? How would you describe the people who are invited to participate in serving in the kingdom of God?

3. Poverty is a global problem. Who are the contributors that you think support and maintain poverty? How do you think poverty affects all of God's creation?

REFLECTION SPACE

Write or express your thoughts or feelings about why being wealthy is desired at the expense of persons starving or having limited food, lack of shelter, and clean water unavailable.

B. The Ten Commandments as a Road Map for Relationships That Honor God

1. God established a relationship of love and freedom with Israel. The Commandments begin with two declarations of God's love for Israel, their response to God, and how they love other people and themselves. Examine Thomas Long's section "God and the Israelites" found in "The Ten Commandments Road Map that Honor God." Select and describe one of the Ten Commandments you understand in Long's explanation that speaks to your relationship with God and others (Thomas Long, "Dancing the Decalogue," Living by the Word, https://www.christiancentury.org/article/2006-03/dancing-decalogue).

2. Draw a map that expresses how three of the Ten Commandments display honor to God. Be creative. You are not limited to only words.

3. How and why does our society hold specific people accountable for not working through their life troubles compared to other racial groups or persons? Share why this dishonors God.

REFLECTION SPACE

Write or express your thoughts or feelings about disrespecting God through idolatry. State one type of idolatry that continues in our lives but dishonors God as written in the Bible. Describe why idolatry keeps a person from living in God's love and justice.

C. A Community of Inclusion, Equality, and Hope

1. The parable of Jesus in Matthew 20:1-7 is a reminder of the invitation extended to all to build God's kingdom. Read verses 8-17 and explain why some workers grumbled and how the owners' responses are similar or not to bootstrap theology.

2. Select a story or movie that focuses on hope despite exclusion. What behaviors or thoughts in your choice resonate with you? Apply the story or movie highlights that speak to hope in times of exclusion and give hope to a historical moment.

3. People are sometimes limited to particular work because of their physical or mental skill level. Explain why you agree or disagree with this statement. When race, gender, and class are factors in persons finding or starting a career, what impact does this have on individuals, their respective communities, the nation, and the world?

REFLECTION SPACE

Write or express your thoughts or feelings on why many Christians choose to ignore the grace Jesus gives to poor or persons different from themselves.

Conclusion

1. Identify one psalm that speaks to your relationship with God's love for all creation.

2. Identify two Scriptures from the Gospels about Jesus' compassion for the oppressed.

3. Identify three reasons why bootstrap theology should be dismantled.

REFLECTION SPACE

Reflect on the issues and pain of unhealthy love. Write a prayer about the blessings of healthy love in your life and the world.